ANOTHER COUNTRY

Carla Carlisle .

III   THE MELODY AT NIGHT

VII   WAY OVER YONDER

Note

The chapters cover 2016 to 2023. The chapter titles are what I listened to at night during those years. I went back in time. I listened to a lot of Janet Baker, Jessye Norman, the Brandenburgs and the Proms but they didn't define the era...

Blowin' In The Wind: Bob Dylan, *The Freewheelin' Bob Dylan;* Tell Me It Isn't True: Bryn Terfel, *Simple Gifts*; The Melody At Night: Keith Jarrett, the whole album, on Repeat; What Ain't To Be Just Might Happen: Dolly Parton, *The Best of Dolly Parton*; I've Enjoyed As Much Of This As I Can Stand: Porter Wagoner's *Greatest Hits*; Sittin' On The Dock Of The Bay: Otis Redding, *The Very Best of Otis Redding;* Way Over Yonder: Carole King, *Tapestry*.

*For Sam and Georgia
and for Ida*

FOREWORD

This comes with a warning. Every one of these essays began with a soft voice beseeching me to 'try and be cheerful'. In truth, the plea to turn on a ray of light for my readers, to kindle a spark in their day, is my every wish. My roots are in the Deep South where they vote for crazy but they love to laugh and they are good at it. Even Faulkner knew that humour absolves the writer of fanaticism, repetition, pedantry and conceit. Most days I'd rather read Nora Ephron than the Booker shortlist, and who doesn't open *Country Life* at the back first and start with Lord and Lady Tottering?

My humour advisor (Reader, I'm married to him) worried that during the years recorded here I'd fractured my funny bone, a break not so serious it required a cast but needing time in a sling. His fears are well-founded. The timeline of these pieces is Brexit, Trump, Boris, Meghan and Harry, a pandemic, and a war in Europe that is closer than it looks.

A further hindrance to my natural hilarity is location. These essays were all written on a mostly arable farm in Suffolk. Farmers are fluent pessimists but nowadays our gloom has horizontal as well as vertical roots. Climate change has put a haze on the meadow, energy prices are high as an elephant's eye, and interest rates are climbing clear up to the sky. The post-Brexit agricultural policy means nobody with a field and a plough has a beautiful feelin' like everything's goin' their way.

* * * *

'Writing is not an occupation,' wrote Sherwood Anderson, the writer and friend who set Hemingway and Faulkner on the writing road. 'When it becomes an occupation a certain amateur spirit is gone out of it. Who wants to lose that?'

Whatever is missing from these pages, I reckon the amateur spirit is intact. My occupation when these pieces were written was running the farm that I had pushed to diversify by planting a vineyard, transforming an ancient barn into a vineyard restaurant and the old dairy into a country store, and adding a bookshop when bookshops were closing faster than pubs, and a weekly farmers' market in the old farmyard. Lodged in my head like a sad song is Isak Dinesen's immortal line 'I had a farm in Africa'.

That's not Southern melodrama. The farms on three sides have been sold in the years I've been here. I never want to start a sentence 'I had a farm in Suffolk'.

* * * *

In case you're wondering, I'm a little embarrassed at introducing another collection. In my defence I only do this every 10 years. That's a long expanse of time to cover in the short space of the essay but it's a form I've liked since I was six years old. Back then I wrote a book I called *The American Way*. It was about alcoholics, drug addicts, kidnapping, Louisa May Alcott and bears. My research was done on the stairs eavesdropping on the grown-ups who thought I was in bed. I have stayed faithful to the form and, considering where I started, I'd say I've lightened up.

I discovered H.L.Mencken in high school, Murray Kempton in college, Ellen Goodman and Erma Bombeck along the way. Hazlitt and Montaigne came after I arrived in England. It was here that I first heard Alistair Cooke's *Letter from America*, and I read and re-read the printed versions of those broadcasts. When I need to sharpen my pen I read the writer Hal Crowther, whose *Cathedrals of Kudzu* is a masterpiece. He's compared to H.L. Mencken but he's better.

However, the everlasting presence in my life is E.B. White. The English know him as the writer of *Charlotte's Web* and *Stuart Little* but Americans know him for the hundreds of pieces he wrote for *The New Yorker* and *Harper's Magazine*. When White left New York City he moved to a saltwater farm in Maine. The writer/farmer sits near me every time I settle down in front of the keyboard. White's deskside partner was Henry David Thoreau. He wrote that Thoreau's themes were 'man's relation to Nature and man's dilemma in society and man's capacity for elevating his spirit'. With Thoreau as his guide, White explained that he would 'beat all this matter together in hope of creating an original omelette from which people can draw nourishment in a hungry day'.

White's hungry days included the Depression, Hitler, the Second World War and the atomic bomb. I count myself lucky that my attempts at providing nourishment haven't included Hitler and Stalin but I take nothing for granted.

Before you go any further I feel honour-bound to admit that I sometimes wrote confidently on matters of which I lacked real insight. I assured readers that Trump would never, ever be elected President of the United States. I wrote that the marriage of Harry and Meghan would contribute lasting hope and joy to the United Kingdom. The week after I wrote that the

English had never appreciated the writer Martin Amis
he received a knighthood. He was on his deathbed but
all the same...

My plan to organise the pieces into themes fell apart
early on. They appear in the order they were written
which, as it turns out, is how life was lived for all of
us during the bewildering years when it felt like the
world had got completely out of hand.

Carla Carlisle

Wyken
July 2023

Only a person who is congenitally self-centred
has the effrontery and the stamina to write essays.
— *E.B. White*

We got to quit running through the briars in
all directions hollering 'Rabbit, rabbit, rabbit!'
and settle on the rabbit we can git.
— *Roy Blount Jr. in 'Long Time Leaving'*

Live or die, live or die, but don't
poison everything…
— *From an early draft of 'Herzog' by Saul Bellow*

I
Blowin' In The Wind

A BANQUET OF CONSEQUENCES

THE morning after the vote, I went to a funeral. It was in the next-door village and everyone was wearing black. No longer the dress code at country funerals, it seemed right to me. Bleary-eyed and overcome with gloom after listening to David Cameron's resignation speech, the sombre tones were comforting, although this farewell was to a woman who never dressed in dull colours.

Actress, theatrical agent and widow of David Croft, who lightened our lives with *Dad's Army*, Ann Croft was the power behind that creative throne. I never saw her without full make-up, luscious pearls, significant diamonds and folds of cashmere as thick as Jersey cream. Glamorous, smart, fond of pleasure and fun, when one of her daughters asked her why she'd had so many children (seven), she replied: 'I kept hoping I'd get one I liked.'

The eulogy by Ian Lavender, the only soldier left of that much-loved rag-tag army, gave us all a lift. He told us that Ann arranged the audition that gave him the life he's had and made him 'Pike' forever. After the service, we walked back to the family home, where we drank Taittinger, the Croft 'house wine', and talked about... well, what else? The Referendum. All Ann's children and grandchildren voted Remain. Worried that she might leave this Earth before she could vote Leave, Ann arranged a postal vote. Her children were not surprised by the result: Ann always got what she wanted.

I spent the rest of the day in a foggy state – a combination of sleeplessness, shock, Champagne and an inbox of 56 emails with the subject heads 'Armageddon / Devastated / Heartbroken / Tragedy/ Apocalypse Now / Moving to Edinburgh'.

Half the emails tried to understand what had brought about this bizarre event in British history. Some dwelt on blame: Ed Miliband, who knifed his brother David in the back and lumbered Labour with Jeremy Corbyn; scurrilous Tory MPs who played Russian roulette with the country; Tony Blair and Gordon Brown, who introduced the Open Borders policy; the all-male cabal of unelected technocrats who sent Mr Cameron back to the UK with his reforms in a paper sack full of holes.

Under the lingering influence of Taittinger, I acquitted all the villains and assigned guilt to Charles de Gaulle, who spent the Second World War in London as a guest of the British Government and repaid that hospitality by fighting for 15 years to keep

Britain and its suspicious penchant for parliamentary democracy out of the European Community.

Searching for blame after the fact is as futile as watching the numbers on the online petition – four million as I write this – calling for a 'cold-feet' referendum. That isn't going to happen. We are where we are. As Robert Louis Stevenson put it: 'Sooner or later everyone sits down to a banquet of consequences.'

Whenever I feel paralysed with confusion, I turn to *The Crack-up*, Scott Fitzgerald's essay, with his formula for restoring sanity: I make lists. In a spirit of generous reconciliation with Leavers, I listed the things about the EU that drove me nuts, but that I'd closed my eyes to. Such as: when the UK became the eighth member state in 1973, the EU accounted for 37% of world economic output – now, with 28 members, it is responsible for barely 17%. And the Leaver's bugbear: the annual accounts that haven't been passed by auditors for 20 years; the absurd pilgrimage to Strasbourg for four days each month just to placate the French; and the tragedies on the coasts of Greece and Italy.

Afraid that I sounded like a UKIP recruit, I started on good things achieved by the EU: the fall of the Berlin Wall (not really an EU achievement, but a great, good thing); the end of dictatorships in Spain and Portugal (ditto); research grants for scientists; agriculture; environment. I then Googled the stirring words from Churchill, speaking at the inaugural

Congress of Europe at The Hague in 1948: 'We must proclaim the mission and design of a United Europe, whose moral conception will win the respect and gratitude of mankind and whose physical strength will be such that none will dare molest her tranquil sway... I hope to see a Europe where men and women of every country will think of being European as of belonging to their native land, and wherever they go in this wide domain will truly feel "here I am at home".'

Inspiring as Churchill's vision is, he did not foresee a world in which millions of Syrian, Afghan, Iraqi and Somalian refugees would flee their homelands. His world did not include the effects of globalisation and climate change. He would not see the camps in Jordan and Turkey.

I'm in as much turmoil now as I was before the referendum. One minute I wish I could turn the clock back, the next I'm ready to fasten my seat belt and endure the turbulence in the belief that it isn't forever.

It's not just markets that crave certainty – people do. In love affairs, business deals, house purchases and degree courses, you just want to know where you stand. The country is more ready for healing than the politicians. Any day now, 'We Want Our Country Back' posters will be graffitied to say: 'We Want Our Lives Back.'

It's a lot easier to forgive if we remember that there

are two sides to this island story. As the dour Scottish undertaker Pte Frazer might have put it: 'Not forgiving is like drinking rat poison and then waiting for the rat to die.'

July 6, 2016

Sooner or later
everyone sits down
to a banquet of
consequences.
Robert Louis Stevenson

SLEEPWALKING TO APOCALYPSE

I'VE always loved the quote from Pauline Kael, film critic on *The New Yorker*, who said: 'I live in a rather special world. I don't personally know anyone who voted for Nixon.' I've thought of her remark a lot lately, because, in my rarefied rural universe, I don't personally know anyone who would vote for Donald Trump. At least, I didn't until a lunch party at which I met an American married to an Englishwoman. Although he's lived in Suffolk for 40 years, he still has a vote in the USA and he's a passionate supporter of Trump. Good grief.

I tuned into the World Service for Trump's acceptance speech, but slept through it and woke up to *Today*'s bone-chilling excerpts from *Apocalypse Now*, a preening, profane Trump telling his gullible followers: 'I am your voice!' He warns that America faces doomsday and 'only I can fix it'.

My first thought was straight from the King James version: 'By the waters of Babylon, there we sat down, yea, we wept, when we remembered Zion.'

I don't come from Republican stock, although my

parents twice voted for Eisenhower. I don't consider the Republican Party America's Zion, but when I think that the party of Lincoln has fallen for a thrice-married, self-promoting demagogue with hair that looks like roadkill, I want to sit down and weep.

Instead of turning to Psalm 137, however, I went to *All the King's Men*. Set in the 1930s, the novel tells the story of the dramatic rise of Willie Stark, a cynical populist who, by sheer force of will, becomes governor of a nameless Southern state. Its author, Robert Penn Warren, denied that it was based on the real-life Huey Long, Louisiana governor and American senator, but anybody born and raised in the shadow of Long country knew better.

It's hard to believe that the messianic Trump isn't from the Deep South. Apocalyptic visions, Calvinist theology, racism and once-upon-a-time visions of a better world (before the Civil War) are in the alluvial soil. The outside world may have thought old Populist evangelism died out with George Wallace, but they were wrong.

When Edwin Edwards, a born-again New Deal Democrat, was running for a third term as governor of Louisiana in 1983, he promised his followers that he would 'Win! Win! And Win Again!'. 'The only way I can lose this election is if I'm caught in bed with either a dead girl or a live boy,' he said. Edwards won four terms, then served eight years in prison – some little thang to do with corruption – but, heck, he's already run for office again.

The difference between Trump and the cankerous Southern Populists is that Trump is a billionaire who was born in Queens, New York, the grandson of German immigrants, and whose Scottish mother was born on the Isle of Lewis. When Trump says that his is the people's voice, he is not a Populist, but a rich man impersonating a Populist. When he tells angry white Americans that foreigners are out to take their jobs, he leaves out the bit that his empire was built on the backs of migrant labour.

His message may proclaim pentecostal egalitarianism, but that doesn't mean every voter gets a Cadillac. His message is that America is sinking deep with the sin of foreigners and terrorists and he alone can fix it, but, after building the wall and declaring a moratorium on Muslims, the well of miracles runs dry. I'm reminded of Roosevelt's Secretary of the Interior Harold Ickes's memorable epithet to Long: 'The gentleman from Louisiana suffers from "halitosis of the intellect".'

Compared with Trump, Long was as worthy as Atticus Finch. Long provided free textbooks to schoolchildren, initiated free night schools for adults, ploughed money into public education, constructed roads and bridges, created public hospitals, and abolished the poll tax that prevented the blacks from voting. He believed that you had to keep religion and race out of politics, but stuck to his belief that 'you can't help the poor whites without helping the Negroes'. True, he turned Louisiana into an almost totalitarian society, censored the press, passed laws determining who could carry guns and scared Roosevelt to death with his plan to rein in millionaires.

November in America is looking more like a referendum than an election. The Trumpers want to leave the big, bad globalised world and cling to the nearly-all-white Leave it to Beaver, a world without immigrants, Muslims, Obamacare and Made in China labels. The rest are the supposedly cultivated, liberal folks who were slow to realise that Trump is not an egomaniacal clown, but someone who got 13 million votes in the Primaries and who could change American politics for the rest of their lives. They are voting to keep the lights on.

It's hard to shake off the words of H. L. Mencken, never over-confident about American democracy, who wrote: 'No one ever went broke underestimating the intelligence of the American voter.'

Here, in the wheat fields of East Anglia, I watch a new Prime Minister who is intelligent and sane. There are deep divisions in this land, but we can celebrate the luxury of a leader with principles, dignity and good hair.*

As for my Trump-loving neighbour, what can I say? You can take a donkey travellin', but it won't come back a horse.

August 3, 2016

---

* That was Theresa May. It didn't turn out well but her dignity, principles and hair remained intact.

A GIDDY EPITHALAMIUM

ON the day that England beat Pakistan by 330 runs in the second Test, we celebrated our 30th wedding anniversary. During the lunch break at Old Trafford, we wandered over to the 400-year-old barn that now houses our vineyard restaurant. Neither of us remembered to book a table, so we celebrated over lunch in the 'first-come, first-served' cafe.

While we waited for our fishcakes, I told my husband about an early poem by Seamus Heaney called *Scaffolding*. The poet persuades his wife that their marriage is good and strong by describing how masons begin a job by testing the scaffolding. They make sure the planks won't slip, the ladders are secure, the bolts are tight. Marital reassurance comes at the poem's end, when the scaffolding comes down: 'We may let the scaffolds fall/Confident we have built our wall.'

Even as I spoke, I could see a distant look in his eyes. Metaphors are to him what cricket scores are to me: infinitely mystifying. But if romantic complicity on this significant day was lacking, I reckon there were three reasons. The wall we've built is still standing (a miracle I take not for granted), the Test match was compelling (to one of us) and, two days later, we were off to Donegal for the wedding of our only son.

Few words are more magical than 'Irish wedding'. Add 'Donegal', 'Fort Stewart' and a rambling Georgian house 'overlooking Lough Swilly', and you have the makings of epithalamia, a vowel-rich word that simply means a poem for a bride or bridegroom, from the Greek *thalmos* or wedding chamber.

I first came across the word through the Scottish poet Roddy Lumsden's poem *On a Promise (An Epithalamium)*, whose wedding is 'A giddy ship/ of fools and family, rocking loose'. We were indeed a giddy ship of family and friends converging on Donegal from a quartet of continents, rocking loose with happiness.

Sam and Georgia met their first week at Edinburgh. What began in friendship turned into romance when she went off to Madrid for her Erasmus year. At least, that's what we thought. Sam made a lot of trips to Spain that year. He did not learn Spanish.

Meanwhile, we practised the discreet charm of parents who long to know everything but don't dare ask. After graduation, Sam grew his own business in London while Georgia went home to Angus, working long hours in a local nursing home while tackling science A-levels and applying to medical school. Her twin sister was already a doctor, but Georgia decided on medicine late. We admired her dedication and sheer grit. When she was offered a place at St Barts, we wept with relief – and tried not to think about the long years of medical training that lay ahead.

Then, a year and a half ago, Sam shyly inquired if I could face parting with my engagement ring, a sapphire heirloom that has graced the left hands of three Carlisle brides. Dizzy with happiness at the thought that Georgia would be the fourth bride, I eagerly slid the ring from my finger – and then heard nothing for months.

Who does not tremble at the words 'Dearly beloved, we are gathered together here in the sight of God, and in the face of this congregation, to join together this Man and this Woman in holy Matrimony'? Who does not shed a tear when listening to vows 'to love and to honour'? And when those brave vows are the prelude to the drama of the joined lives of an only son and a young woman with two sisters, a brother and 22 first cousins, it truly feels like Eureka.

The bride entered on the arm of her father to the same cello music by Nigel Hess that I walked down the aisle to with my father 30 years earlier. The homily was by the couple's close friend Tim, now studying for the priesthood. It was his first wedding. The Celebrant was the same Irish priest who married Simon and Katy, parents of the bride, in 1985. Back then, it was Father Carney's first wedding service. At the signing of the register, Lucinda May, wife of Tim, sang *Down to the River to Pray*, probably a first in St Mary's Church in Ramelton. When we signed our register, three decades earlier, Jill Gomez sang *Steal Away* and *Deep River*, a first for the crypt chapel in the Palace of Westminster. A marriage tapestry; something old, something new.

Husband and wife left the church on the back of a tractor, symbolic transport for a country wedding. The reception was at the family home, which really does overlook Lough Swilly. The Dessain family and extended cousinage spent the weeks before painting the barn, creating the swags that hung from the high windows and making sure everything worked. The bride's mother grew all the flowers and made the wedding cake. The bridegroom shot the pesky Wyken muntjac and made the *carpacchio* of venison. We drank Wyken Moonshine, the sparkling wine from our vineyard.

The speeches were gentle and profound, loving and fun. The bride's sisters sang, Euan performed his wedding song on the bagpipes, whippets Hester and Luna were elegant and photogenic, and velvety young bullocks, posing on the shore like well-fed extras in a romantic film, now feature on iPhones around the world. Fortified by draught Guinness, we danced until dawn.

Of course, everyone said that the greatest good luck

was the weather: the sun shone all day, shafts of light landing on emerald-green fields like a sudden grace. Which brings me to the last lines of my favourite epithalamium, Alice Oswald's poem *Wedding*: 'and when the luck begins, it's like a wedding,/which is like love, which is like everything.'

September 7, 2016

16

IN THE LAND OF WISHFUL THINKING

IT'S been a quiet autumn here in the Land of Wishful Thinking, twinned in our hearts with Lake Wobegon, where 'all the women are strong, the men are good looking; and all the children are above average'. Maybe it comes from being surrounded by wheat fields and sugar beet, but ours is a place where common sense prevails.

In the Land of Wishful Thinking, all the dogs are loyal and good-natured. They are also registered and wear a dog tag to prove it. We pay £10 per dog, but for that our hound gets a chip. The cats all have bells round their necks and, I'm glad to say, the songbirds are back and singing again.

Everybody who drives around here carries their driving licence when they're behind the wheel, just like in Lake Wobegon – in fact, like everywhere else in the world. It's an instant identity card without all the expense and bureaucracy of identity cards, and it saves a lot of time if there's an accident. We also keep our insurance papers in the car at all times, and the little paper car licence is back on the windscreen because getting rid of it was a big, expensive mistake. Admitting mistakes is the badge of common sense, so we don't mind doing it.

In the Land of Wishful Thinking, all the houses are designed for human habitation. We brought back the old Parker Morris standards, which decreed that all rooms had to be a minimum size. The developers huffed and puffed about that, but nobody is proud of the fact that Britain is building the smallest new houses in Europe. A kitchen ought to be big enough to have a table, a bedroom needs a bedside light, and putting people in rabbit hutches makes them crazy. We've also put a moratorium on David Cameron's Right to Buy policy. We reckon that was a mistake, 'cause we're pretty short of houses in these parts.

In the Land of Wishful Thinking, you now have to be resident in the country for five years before you're allowed to own property. We're grateful to Denmark for that idea. It's annoyed folks who want to get their money out of dubious countries and see property in Britain as an investment, but, frankly, we don't give a damn. We have a pretty poor opinion of ghost towns and absentee owners.

In the Land of Wishful Thinking, most children go to the local schools, which are pretty good. Home schooling is closely monitored, and parents who want to do it have to pass an exam that is tougher than the 11-plus. The way we look at it, teaching is a hard job and should be left to the folks who are dedicated and trained.

I have to admit that there are no longer any badgers in the Land of Wishful Thinking, but the cows are free of TB, and the hedgehogs and the bees have made a miraculous comeback. We got fed up with the supermarkets screwing the dairy farmers, so we brought back milk in bottles, delivered to our front door. The milk is from the local Jersey herd, and seeing cows in the fields makes us all happy.

The churches in the Land of Wishful Thinking are no longer derelict since we got rid of VAT on repairs. That tax really was a dumb mistake. We also transformed the churches from being bat sanctuaries into real sanctuaries, and we spearheaded a movement to sponsor Christian refugee families – one family for every five parishes. We got that idea from Canada. We wish we'd done it sooner.

The local surgery has diet and exercise classes two nights a week because some of us aren't the size we used to be. The local library holds free English classes two nights a week and a book club/pot-luck supper one evening a month.

The local GPs were amazed when we did away with parking charges at the local hospital. They agreed with us: paying when you're sick or visiting the sick is no way to finance the NHS. We think that idea's time had come.

By now, you may be thinking that the Land of Wishful Thinking is nostalgic and provincial, but our hearts beat with hopes and dreams beyond these wheat fields. We're a long way from Hinkley Point, but we hope it will never be built by the Chinese. Common sense says, if it's really worth building – and not a big, expensive mistake – we should do it ourselves.

Ditto HS2. We love trains in the Land of Wishful Thinking, but we think it's pig-headed and ignorant to rip up the countryside in order to shave 20 minutes off the journey between Birmingham and London. What we want are better trains, not faster trains. As for that third runway at Heathrow, we're on the side of the folks who live, work and pay taxes in London. We think they should be able to sleep and breathe. Sleeping and breathing shouldn't be wishful thinking.

Politicians tell us that folks in the Land of Wishful Thinking live in a dream world. They mutter about green papers, and say that much depends on the Chinese, market forces, the bat lobby and the banks. We say that it's wishing that allows us to hope, and hope has wings. Or something like that.

I do know this: we who dwell in the Land of Wishful Thinking have an unstoppable will to make real that which others only dream of. We're here to stay.

October 5, 2016

THE ART OF MAKING POSSIBLE

I DON'T like to think I am frivolous and vain, but, lately, I've been quietly revising my image of myself. It's been a humbling exercise.

The acute phase of this self-examination began in April 2015 when, after two years of coy denials, Hillary Rodham Clinton announced she would seek the Presidency of the USA. I watched that broadcast three times. I marvelled at the grit, the resilience, the rock-hard determination and the staggering energy of the woman. I looked at her skin, which glowed. I studied the teeth that are as straight and even as sweetcorn in August. And her hair: thick, healthy, golden. I may have heard something about 'stronger together', but I was thinking: what a great cut! What a genius of a colourist! There is not a woman in the world I have watched grow older and blonder with such compulsive scrutiny.

It's a slender claim to fame, but Hillary Rodham and I once had the same hair: long and mouse brown with a centre parting as straight as the line down the middle of the highway. I know this because I have grainy black-and-white photographs of us at about the same time, in June 1969. Although we are several hundred miles apart, we are doing the same thing: speaking at our college commencement, mine the progressive Sarah Lawrence College in New York, hers the traditional Wellesley in Massachusetts.

It was the decade of civil rights, Vietnam, assassinations and what was called 'student unrest'. Our positions behind the podiums were the result of petitions 'requesting' the right to speak at our graduation ceremonies. Martin Luther King and Robert Kennedy had been dead barely a year, and all the young men gathering were nervously looking for ways to avoid the draft (including Bill Clinton, George Bush, Mitt Romney and the present Republican candidate who got a deferment for 'bad feet').

My speech began with Bertolt Brecht's *To Posterity* with its beginning 'A smooth forehead betokens/a hard heart' and its plaintive ending 'Do not judge us/Too harshly'. I explained – at what my father described as 'Apostolic length' – that my generation 'finds no value or stability in a country where there is increasing poverty in the midst of increasing wealth... which gives priority to ABM [anti-ballistic missiles] while it closes poverty centres, job programmes, libraries, hospitals... a country that values money more than it values the lives of its people'.

Hillary's speech also included poetry: 'All we can do is keep trying again and again. There's that wonderful line in *East Coker* about there's only the trying, again and again and again; to win again what we've lost before.' Nearly 50 years on, it seems prophetic. As does the poem she ended with, by her classmate Nancy Schreiber: 'And you and I must be free/Not to save the world in a glorious crusade/Not to kill ourselves with a nameless gnawing pain/But to practise with all the skill of our being/The art of making possible.'

I didn't know Hillary, but we almost met the following September. We had both secured a place at Yale Law School, two of the 28 women in a class of 235. Between applying and acceptance, however, I'd begun to doubt that I had the orderly brain of a lawyer. I was also inspired by a community organiser called Saul Alinsky; I decided to work for change 'outside the system', and went to California to work in factories that were points of production for the war. I had the hazy notion that, if the workers refused to produce napalm, defoliates, detonators and M16 rifles, the war would end. A 'glorious crusade' indeed.

My attempts at anti-war consciousness-raising got me elected shop steward of the Oil, Chemical and Atomic Workers International Union, which was the beginning and ending of my electoral career. My fellow workers, many who'd gone west in search of work during the Dust Bowl era and the Second World War, were cynical about the war in Asia, but had no quarrel with capitalism – they owned houses, cars and motor boats. Their lives were rooted in reality, not theory. I slowly became less convinced of 'theory' myself. After a year of packing defoliates, Glen Campbell and Johnny Cash had more resonance for me than Marx and Hegel.

Although I voted for Bill Clinton (twice), I was unaware of my tentative connection with Hillary until my father arrived one Christmas and slid a manila envelope under the tree. The card read 'Souvenirs of The Road Not Taken'. Inside were newspaper clippings from the *New York Times* showing that, once, Hillary and I were marching to the beat of the same drum. She even wrote her senior thesis at Wellesley on Saul Alinsky.

I have to admit that I haven't always been an uncritical fan. We finally met when she was running for Senator for the state of New York. I admired her for advocating engagement, not disruption or 'revolution', but I was sceptical. When she ran for President in 2007, I hitched my wagon to a star called Obama. It seemed as close to the good revolution as I would see in my lifetime. But now I find myself a genuine admirer of this woman who is a liberal pragmatist, a disciplined lawyer and, I'm tempted to say, a 'soul sister', the one who got the good hair. She is smart enough to understand that Donald Trump's appeal can't be dismissed. She recognises that there is a deep and troubling divide in America, and there is no health in it.

On November 8, barring a cataclysmic event*, Hillary Clinton will become the first woman US President. The relief will pass all understanding, relief around the world that goes beyond the nihilism of a Trump presidency. And 'somewhere ages and ages hence', I might, like Robert Frost, be telling this with a sigh: 'Two roads diverged in a wood, and I –/I took the one less travelled by,/And that has made all the difference.'

I can live with that.

November 2, 2016

---

* We all know how that ended. A cataclysmic event that stunned the world, and still makes me mad and sad.

WHAT COMES NEXT...

HERE on the Suffolk prairies, the death of Fidel Castro has mostly gone unnoticed. There are no Cuban refugees in Bury St Edmunds, although there are probably some third-generation Cuban-Americans stationed at Lakenheath, the American base 45 minutes from here. Still, the news switched on one of those home movies that reside in the back of my mind.

My mental newsreel of the Cuban Missile Crisis is easily retrieved because we had daily drills at my elementary school in case the Russian missiles stationed 200 miles from the American coastline came our way. We had plenty of reason to be scared because any missiles aimed at Washington or New York had to go right over our Mississippi heads.

My main memory of those 'duck and cover' exercises was the discovery of crops of chewing gum stuck underneath the desks, grey wads the size of the ticks we pulled from our dogs. I was a squeamish child, and my disgust outweighed my fear. My other memory was the bomb shelter built a year earlier by our neighbours, the Rileys. My parents were scathing about this shelter. My father's approach to the end of civilisation was to buy a couple of cases of Jim Beam and store them in the gun closet. He made no provision for his children, unlike Mr Riley, who thought of everything.

Visits to the bomb shelter were forbidden, but their son Jim knew where the key was kept. We would sneak down and gaze in wonder at the neat rows of flashlights, lanterns, matches, tins of tuna fish, Vienna sausages and pineapple chunks, Cheerios, Graham crackers and powdered milk, a stack of *National Geographics*, a metal first-aid cabinet and shelves of bottled water and Dr Pepper.

The Rileys were Baptists, so there was no bourbon, but there were two bunk beds, a crank that would provide ventilation, and two buckets with a bag of lime in a corner. 'That's the bathroom,' Jim told me. This was long before I read Anne Frank's diary, but the shelter had an addictive spookiness. One day, I noticed a shotgun propped up in the corner. 'Is that to shoot the Russians?' 'Nope,' came Jim's solemn reply. 'It's to shoot the people who try to get in here. All the folks who don't have a bomb shelter.' I must have got the message because I never went back.

The Cuban Missile Crisis lasted only 13 days, and the rage for bomb shelters wound down after a couple of years. All the same, it's pathetic irony that the unrepentant Castro is departing his earthly revolution as President-Elect Donald Trump takes office. Castro tried to turn his small island into a continent, and Mr Trump wants to turn his hunk of continent into an island. Without Fidel hovering in Havana, however, I'm less worried about Mr Trump's threats to overturn Obama's restoration of diplomatic relations between Cuba and the USA after five decades: 'Obama got a bad deal! I could've got a much better deal!'

The President-Elect has already checked out sites for 'Trump Cubana', and I suspect he'll quietly ignore the resentful elderly Cuban-Americans who gave him their vote. If I read that Trump buys Guantanamo Bay, bulldozes it to the ground and builds Mar-a-Lago II, I won't think it's 'fake news'.*

I've now had nearly a month to get used to the idea of a President Trump. Thank you for asking, but, no, I'm not feeling better as time passes. I've listened to Radio 4's *Letters from America* and *Points of View* and read thousands of words about how Trump heard 'the voice of forgotten Americans' but Hillary listened to Beyoncé and Cher; how Trump held mass rallies in the Rust Belt, but Hillary held fundraisers in Hollywood. I feel like an earthquake victim who can hear the radio but can't hear the voices of rescuers.

The truth is that neither candidate was good enough. I realised that when the black church in

---

* I got that wrong. Trump has stuck with the Cuban-Americans in Florida who don't want any more Cubans coming in.

Greenville, Mississippi, was set ablaze and large white letters painted on the side read 'Vote Trump'. I didn't expect him to show up (he visited the state a couple of months earlier at an all-white rally with Nigel Farage), but I wish Hillary had.

My friend Raymond emailed from Dublin: 'Robert Kennedy would have cancelled his schedule, headed south and given the members of the burned-out church and the country the two things missing from this campaign: comfort and eloquence.' Remembering Kennedy's words on the campaign trail – 'that human history is shaped each time someone stands up for an ideal or acts to improve the lot of others or strikes out against injustice' – makes the absence of grace and ideals in this campaign feel even sadder.

I'm more embarrassed than terrified that this petulant narcissist will have the nuclear code in his pocket. I also realise that my liberal elitist's bomb shelter – a wine cellar with a few good bottles and the last case of whisky my father-in-law bought before the 1983 Budget – might not get me through the four years ahead. I'll add to it – two stacks of *Country Life* and a box of candles – as soon as I finish the book that arrived this morning. Called *What Comes Next and How to Like It*, it's a meditation on ageing, family, dogs and life's woes. I'll let you know if it works.

December 7, 2016

II

Tell Me It Isn't True

NEW YEAR, LAST WORDS

WHEN I headed upstairs this morning, mug of coffee in hand, my husband had only six words to say to me: 'Try not to write about Trump.'

This was an ancient echo. Half a century ago, my grandmother's plea after reading every word I wrote was: 'Can't you write something cheerful? Take pity on this gloomy old world.'

In fact, this Christmas was a miracle of cheerfulness and joy. The house was full, rocking to the rhythm of cooking, eating, drinking, walking and singing. For five whole days I stopped reading newspapers as though they were a black box recovered from a crash site and would explain how one country's flight went so wrong.

Then, as soon as the last car was loaded and final farewells and hugs were made, the lacuna of time that hovers over the arrival of a new year descended. This is usually a meditative time. The house is empty, but the larder is half full. The tree still smells of Maine, and in this age of genetic miracles the needles are hanging on.

On every significant surface of the house is a crèche (the English call it a crib, which sounds less poetic to my ear), including a wooden one whittled in the hills of Kentucky, and another in granite resin sculpted by French nuns, who take a vow of silence and spend their lives creating figures that are sold in cathedral shops.

It takes me a whole day to bring every Mary, Joseph, Infant Christ, shepherds, Wise Men, donkeys and sheep from the attic. I begin in daylight with *St Matthew Passion* and tea, and end at dusk with Ella Fitzgerald and eggnog. I like to get maximum spiritual bang for my buck, so these Nativity *tableaux* remain in place long past Epiphany.

This year, however, another thought wandered through my mind as I assembled the figures: who will do this in the misty future when I'm not around? Should I take pictures with my phone? Leave stage directions? My new daughter-in-law is in her fourth year studying medicine at Barts; her twin sister, now a junior doctor, was on duty in a Kent hospital, and only arrived in Suffolk the night of Christmas Day. We reversed Boxing Day and Christmas Day so all she missed was The Queen's Speech. Their future lives do not suggest whole days to set up heirloom Nativity scenes.

But the thought that the tradition of the crèches might go with me (that same grandmother liked to warn us, 'I might die someday; 10 out of 10 do') has lingered with me during this festive season, despite the fact that I haven't got a single ache and suffer nothing more worrying than thinner hair and the odd fog that descends over names.

Still, the decision to photograph the Nativity scenes triggered the desire to create order. I realised my will needed an update and the addition of passwords and PINs. I looked at my list of wishes. Treasures I considered precious 10 years ago now seem shabby. I also detected a new attitude. I felt like giving away a lot of the 'good' stuff now. Not in an effort to swindle the taxman out of probate, although that's a thought, but for the satisfaction of giving while the giving feels good.

All this preparation for the new year felt like a higher realm of clearing my clutter, but then I went a step further: I decided to write my memorial service. Inspired by a trilogy of funerals in Advent, it felt practical to put pen to paper while I still have my marbles and can remember what I like. This takes more time than you'd think, and my husband was mystified by my morbid determination. He was also relieved to think that, should I go first, he wouldn't have to worry about getting it right.

As with my will, I reckon I will revise this document regularly. Once, I wanted a wicker coffin, but now I think they are noisy and look like laundry baskets. The wool ones made in Yorkshire look heavenly, but they also resemble hatboxes. I've settled on a dark green, almost black, cardboard coffin with or without rope handles (note: handles on all coffins are purely decorative, expensive and unnecessary).

It's possible that what I've written looks more like a concert than a farewell service, but I'm with Sir Thomas Browne, physician of Norwich, who wrote: 'Happy are they that go to bed with grand music.' I've even ordered the sheet music so no one has to scramble around for it. 'Don't worry,' my son assures me, 'it's all available on YouTube.'

When I finally finished on New Year's Eve, I tenderly placed my *memento mori* in one of those nice paisley boxes from OKA. I felt inexpressibly serene. I also felt it was a generous gift to those left behind – well, maybe not the musical requirements (Copland, Britten, Brahms' clarinet concerto), but I hope I'll leave a wad sufficient to fund musicians.

There is one small problem. In this house, we spend a great deal of time searching for important papers, so I've left copies in the gun safe, the drinks cupboard, various desks and drawers, plus a file on my computer entitled 'Last Words'. Oh, thoughtful me.

With the peace that passes all understanding, I'm ready for the life that comes. I vow not to slip photographs of the crèche arrangements in the back of the box in the years to come. Now, I simply await praise: this page has been triumphantly – almost – Trump-free.

January 4, 2017

THE OPTIMIST'S DAUGHTER

LET me say from the start that I don't believe that people who read are more socially competent and personally effective, more self-reliant and trustworthy, less likely to go to pieces under stress, more moral and kinder than people who read only Twitter, text messages and street signs.

I do tend to think that readers are more likely to be able to communicate their ideas and ideals. Indeed, they are more likely to have ideals and convictions that come from experience, but are honed from books. Some books are good, some are great, some disappointing, some trashy, some unforgettable. Books, like life, are a lottery, but, as a recent American President admitted, in his sometimes lonely youth they were 'worlds that were portable'. Books were the companions that helped him to figure out who he was, what he thought and what was important.

My belief in and love of books may be wildly disproportionate to the important things in life, but I reckon my indebtedness to the printed word is exceeded only by my debt to my parents for giving me the DNA of a bookworm. They were both readers in a dry state, in which the only bookshop was the Baptist Bookstore in a town 85 miles away. Like the bourbon they also enjoyed, books had to be acquired in New Orleans as well as from the Book of the Month Club. The town library was a peaceable kingdom, but the librarians were self-made censors who withheld books they judged 'not quite right', which meant anything by John Steinbeck, F. Scott Fitzgerald or Ernest Hemingway. I was saved by Louisa May Alcott, who revealed to me that there were two sides to the Civil War.

Times are turbulent enough without inflicting another diatribe on my faithful readers, so I may be pushing my luck when I suggest that the new American President's gravest flaw, perhaps the origin of all his flaws, is that he does not read. I wasn't surprised to learn that he hadn't made his way through a book from start to finish since high school. Then came the revelation from Marie Brenner in *Vanity Fair*, verified by ghost-writers, ex-wives and fastidious fact-checkers, that on his bedside table (to be fair, in the bedside drawer) was a volume of Hitler's speeches. Wherever you stand on the political divide, this is a heck more troubling than a refusal to produce tax returns.

At times in my life, I have used books to shut out the real world. I'll always be grateful that my drug of choice during adolescence was literature: Daphne du Maurier, Sinclair Lewis (*Main Street*'s Carol Kennicott made me a lifelong idealist, but also determined not to live my life in Gopher Prairie). Somewhere between *Middlemarch* and *The Golden Notebook*, I decided my spiritual home was England, but it was the 19th-century Romantics who got me here: an assignment to write a television series based on their exhilarating, rebellious, melancholy and brave lives. I am forever grateful to Byron, Keats, Wordsworth, Shelley and Coleridge.

If it was English literature that gave me the 'nose' and the instincts of a gun dog that follows the wild turkey across the swamp, it was Southern literature that I turned to once I lived in England. When you are a child of the Mississippi Delta, William Faulkner's fictionalised county Yoknapatawpha (the accent is on 'taw'; it's a Chickasaw Indian word meaning 'water runs slow through flat land') was too close in time and place to reality. Now that I live in the flatlands of East Anglia, reading Eudora Welty is like waking up in my own bed after a long journey.

My '*Desert Island*' book would be the Library of America volume of Welty's novels. It includes her masterpiece, *The Optimist's Daughter*, the story of a young woman who rediscovers the world of her Southern childhood when she returns home to be with her dying father. When I first read it, I couldn't understand the 'optimism' of a father who would leave the family home to his new young wife and not his daughter. It took a second reading, years later, to see that his legacy to his daughter was an understanding of the meaning of life and the values that were formed and nourished inside the house.

Critics of Barack Obama accused him of being aloof, too intellectual. Those critics won't miss the poetry and the mastery of language in speeches that evoked the King James Bible, Shakespeare, the Declaration of Independence, Abraham Lincoln and Martin Luther King. I will miss the optimism that comes from a view of the world that attaches the mule of language to the wagon of history. I'll miss the President who gives his daughter a Kindle filled with books he wants to share with her. I'll miss the President who said that Shakespeare's plays show the human condition entirely: 'Its follies, cruelties, and mad blunders, but also its resilience, decencies and acts of grace.'

Tempting as it is to spend the next four years hunkered down, reading books on my bedside table that have got stuck there and re-reading old friends that make me feel better, I know that this is no time to retreat to the shelter of a world that allows entry only to the likeminded. More than ever, now is the time to challenge the all-pervasive, dystopian view of the world – everything is terrible and will only get worse – that frightens voters and makes them crazy.

I think it is my (our) job to preach the gospel of

optimism, even on days when it feels deluded. These *are* the good old days – they're the only days we've got. It is history, written in plays, novels, poetry, even *Country Life*, that teaches us to hope. Water runs slow through flat land, but we need to keep faith. And keep reading.

February 1, 2017

GALLOPING ABOUT DOING GOOD

DESPITE the new gospel of sleep as salvation, my alarm is set for *Farming Today*. This would be a sensible way to begin the day if I kept farmers' hours. I don't. I'm still up at 11.30pm, so I rarely miss *Poetry Please*. Roger McGough is like an old friend; his soft voice is as peaceful and exciting as a well-aged Pauillac. He's been especially on song lately, what with an evening of 'Poems for Dark Days' followed by a whole evening of Philip Larkin. I'm not a woman who's only happy when she's sad, but Larkin's pessimism cheers me up.

I was surprised when *This be the Verse* was read with nary a bleep the other night. True, it was midnight and listeners were forewarned of 'strong language', but it was a relief to hear the poem we know by heart read without being censored. Another poem everyone knows almost by heart is Stevie Smith's *Not Waving but Drowning*. It feels timely, as a lot of us are discovering we are much 'further out than we thought'.

The poetry of Smith of Palmers Green was a revelation after years of reading Sylvia Plath, who wrote in her journal that she was 'hooked on Smith's poetry', and the equally troubled Robert Lowell, who turned to Smith on grey days to enjoy 'her unique and cheerfully gruesome voice'.

These days, however, the Smith poem I can't get out of my head is *The Galloping Cat*. It begins: 'Oh I am a cat that likes to/Gallop about doing good.' Alas, the cat creates havoc, and then blames the unpleasant results on irritating angels: 'What's the good of galloping about doing good/When angels stand in the path/And do not do as they should.'

I know the feeling. I, too, like to gallop about doing good. My notion of 'good' is not tenderly caring for the sick and the poor; it's closer to the Thatcherite doctrine (conceived long before I'd heard of Thatcher) that everyone is happier if they have something of their own. Even in my days of Tolstoyan dreaminess, I never believed that collective farming would make people as happy as ploughing their own furrow. As soon as marriage provided a significant plot of my own, I began galloping about putting my good intentions into practice.

Ten years ago, when farming was going through a tricky period, I proposed to Will, who farms our land, that he might supplement his income with an egg-laying business. I suggested the five-acre field next to woodland as a paradise for free-range chickens. The restaurant would buy his eggs, and the rest could be sold at our weekly farmer's market. His wife, Emma, designed chicken houses that looked like shepherd's huts, and together they created a thriving business. A couple of years later, they bought a 30-acre field three miles away and created a more viable free-range egg farm.

When Will's assistant manager, Kris, wanted to start an asparagus business, I was delighted. We rented him a field, and last year the first crop of his Wyken asparagus was served in restaurants throughout Suffolk. Charles, our vineyard manager, has a business selling 'trees for gardens', which surround the old bull pen and enhance the farmyard car park.

Praise be the cat who gallops about spreading happiness and prosperity. Except, as the cat points out: 'Galloping about doing good/Is a full-time job/That needs/An experienced eye of earthly Sharpness.'

My earthly sharpness did not foresee that something called H5N8 virus – bird flu – would invade this happy utopia on the wings of a dove and on wings of ducks and geese from Siberia. Although my own mixed choir of chickens, turkeys, peacocks and guinea fowl has been shut up in the fruit cages since December, my sadness at its imprisonment is trivial compared with the sleepless nights now endured by Will and Emma.

I have 12 hens; they have 12,000 free-range birds. My hens, peace-loving Dark Brahmas who lay only when the spirit moves them, contribute to my pleasure, but not my livelihood. Will and Emma's birds represent their life savings and a decade of hard work. So far, their birds have accepted their confinement with grace, but, as the days grow longer, they will express their dismay by laying less. Supermarkets are already dropping the premium for free-range eggs and insisting on paying the 'barn egg' price, although the enhanced welfare for confined birds is eating into the farmer's income.

Just as we were hoping that the birds would resume their free-range lives, a seventh case of bird flu was confirmed, in Redgrave, Suffolk, 10 miles from Will and Emma's farm. Some birds died and the remaining 23,000 were culled. You could say that the Redgrave farm was a sitting target. It's a stone's throw from Redgrave Fen, a nature reserve that attracts wild birds on their migratory journeys from Siberia. Or you might have thought, 'what an idyllic setting for free-range chickens who help provide the nicest of the 34 million eggs a day that we eat in Britain'.

I hate to think that I may have led Will and Emma into a business that could be devastating. I would advise fellow cats galloping about doing good that it's a bit more complicated.

I should add that the 'Dark Days' of *Poetry Please* referred to winter, not political or moral times. But that's what I love about poetry: double meanings. It's worth clicking on to iPlayer if you missed it. The poem by Emily Dickinson might reassure: 'Hope is the thing with feathers/That perches in the soul/And sings the tune without the words/And never stops at all.' Hope. Feathers. Galloping about doing good. Poetry. Please.

March 1, 2017

A TALE OF FRIENDSHIP
AND PRINTER'S INK

IN this age of spiritual doubt, I confess that my one steadfast belief is in the power of the printed word. Newspapers and magazines may be on an economic cliff edge (this one excepted), and fake news the scourge of our time, but there is still something solemn and significant about thoughts in print. I'd even suggest that the printed page is transformative. In the years I occupied the back page of *Country Life* I was certain that my words weighed more in print than they did on my screen. The power of printer's ink also had another magical effect: friendship.

A column I wrote in praise of E. B. White led to a letter from readers in America – they had bought the writer's homestead in Brooklin, Maine. Would I like to stay there? We organised a swap: they began their English trip with us, and then we took off for Maine. It's a friendship that lives on.

Another friend I owe to *Country Life* is Bob Michell. OrAlastair Robert Michell, BVetMED, DSc,

FRSA, MRCVS. One Saturday at the farmer's market, an attractive woman came up to me and said: 'My husband is a regular reader of yours.' The husband was a safe distance away, and what I took for shyness turned out to be modesty.

I joined them for coffee, and learned that Bob was a vet and that he, too, wrote a column, 'Speculum', for *Veterinary Times*. I begged for copies, and my persistence paid off. Without them I'd never have learned that this 'vet' held a personal chair in comparative medicine from the University of London, first at the Royal Veterinary College, latterly at Barts, was president of the RVVS, on the Addenbrooke's board of governors, and a recipient of the most distinguished prizes in his field.

That first morning, however, I learned only that he and Pauline had spent a year in New York, where Bob did research for his PhD, and another two years on a Harkness Fellowship in Santa Monica, California.

Attached to the first batch of columns was a note explaining that, early on, he'd dispensed with the need to find a veterinary 'hook', although, at times – during the foot-and-mouth tragedy, for instance – he combined his fury and his scientific knowledge with the clarity and passionate conscience of Darwin and Pasteur.

Over the years, I joined them for a drink whenever they came to the vineyard for lunch. We shared politics and music, writers and books, and I was pleased to surprise him with a couple of volumes by the critic

John Leonard, whom they knew in their New York days. Then, one hot summer day, Bob took me aside and told me that Pauline had been diagnosed with pancreatic cancer. Seven months later she died.

After Pauline's death, Bob moved to Oxfordshire to be near his daughter. Happily for me, his erudite and original columns still arrived. Over time, he had written about assisted dying – the first one in my 'Michell Archive' is dated November 2001, written after a joint meeting between the Royal Society of Medicine and the New York Academy of Medicine on the subject of 'Ethical Dilemmas at the Beginning and End of Life'. It was my introduction to a belief that Bob felt strongly: that human medicine needs to learn from the humanity of animal medicine.

He returned to the subject in June 2013, describing the moment in his wife's illness when the palliative care that had achieved miracles had gone beyond the reach of its effectiveness. Twice she asked him for the tenderness and mercy that had been shown to their black lab two years earlier when the dog had suffered a stroke. 'Undoubtedly, had there just been the two of us, I could not have refused her pleas, but I didn't want our daughter to have a court case as well as a bereavement.' He added: 'If such pain was inflicted on a laboratory rat, it would be illegal. If an animal in my care was allowed to suffer like this, I would receive a complaint, discipline, even being struck off.'

One of Bob's last columns begins: 'There is one

disease of the heart that is understood better by writers and musicians than by scientists: grief. It's like being at sea without a compass.' The rich memories of nearly 50 years of happy marriage, a beloved daughter, Tania, three loving grandchildren and the affection of the young lab Pauline left behind couldn't dislodge the agony of Bob's grief. 'Rationality has little to contribute,' he writes, and quotes Joan Didion: 'Grief turns out to be a place none of us know until we reach it... we might expect that we will be crazy with loss: we do not expect to be literally crazy.'

On March 10, friends, family and colleagues said farewell to Bob in a memorial service in a beautiful chapel next to Dulwich College, where he went to school. In the end, Bob's grief was more than he could or wanted to bear.

I am lucky to have known this remarkable man. Thanks to the printed word, it was a friendship that covered more terrain than we would ever have managed in a few short meetings. And, thanks to my blue box labelled 'Speculum', I have the reward and comfort of a big heart and a very good mind.

April 5, 2017

ODE TO BILLIE JOE

IF I say 'Tallahatchie River', somewhere in the southern hemisphere of your mind you might recall *Ode to Billie Joe*. You might hear those opening lines: 'It was the third of June, another sleepy, dusty Delta day/I was out choppin' cotton and my brother was balin' hay.' You may even remember the boy and girl who 'threw something off the Tallahatchie Bridge' better than you recall the song's main theme: 'Billie Joe McAllister jumped off the Tallahatchie Bridge.'

I was born in that hot, dusty delta, and our fields rolled down to the Tallahatchie – Choctaw Indian word for 'rock of waters'. When the song came out it felt as if Bobbie Gentry had put our moonscape of cotton and soy beans on the map. Her husky voice and the hypnotic beat mystified her fans, who wanted to know just one thing: what was thrown off the bridge before Billie Joe jumped off? A ring? A gun? A baby?

I always thought the lyrics had a major flaw: it was unlikely that Billie Joe's plunge would have been fatal. The bridge was low and the river was slower. The shock of hitting the water would remind a man of something worse than his troubles: the water moccasins, poisonous snakes that thrive in the muddy river. In real life, Billie Joe would have swum to the bank and re-evaluated his death wish.

By the time the song had dislodged The Beatles' *All You Need Is Love* as number one, I was a rare Southern voice at a New England women's college and didn't feel inclined to show off my Tallahatchie insider knowledge. I listened in amazement as my literature professor compared the song to *Romeo and Juliet*, and a Hegel scholar described it as a polemic on abortion. An article in the Yale student paper claimed that Billie Joe jumped because he'd been drafted, a more convincing theory in 1967 when Lyndon Johnson announced he was sending 45,000 more troops to Vietnam.

Just as speculation died down, a radical lawyer claimed that Billie Joe jumped into the river because he was the son of one of the men guilty of the kidnapping and lynching 12 years earlier of the 14-year-old black boy Emmett Till. Problem was, Billie Joe was fiction; Emmett Till was not.

Memory is transient and it fluctuates, but I think August 1955 is when I began to suspect that 'fake news' is like *kudzu*, the vine in the South that eventually smothers every living thing. I was eight when Emmett Till's body was pulled out of a bend in

51

the Tallahatchie called Pecan Point, the spot where my grandfather taught me to bait my hooks with chicken necks and angle for catfish. A boy was fishing there on that August morning when he saw what looked like a dark foot poking out of the water.

Emmett Till's crime? Like me, he was visiting relatives. He'd gone with his cousins to hang out at a country store in Money, Mississippi. He went inside to buy some gum, and allegedly flirted with a white woman, Carolyn Bryant, whose husband owned the store. According to FBI transcripts released in 2007, when Mrs Bryant left the store to get a gun from her car Emmett let out a 'wolf whistle'.

Within hours of his disappearance, folks swore they'd seen 'the boy' get on a train in Greenwood and that he was back in Chicago with his mama. The local newspapers insisted the whole thing was a plot by 'outside agitators' to bring disgrace on Mississippi. Claims that he'd drowned while swimming only evaporated when the police revealed that he was found with an iron fan tied to his neck with barbed wire.

In the end, Mississippi brought disgrace on itself. The trial of Mrs Bryant's husband and his half-brother ended in an all-white jury finding them innocent. A few months later, they confessed their guilt in a story for *Look* magazine, but double jeopardy meant they couldn't be tried again for the same crime. They collected $4,000 for their story.

Carolyn Bryant is still alive, and 10 years ago

agreed to talk to the historian Timothy Tyson. She told him that the crucial piece of her testimony was untrue, that Till never 'grabbed her around the waist and uttered obscenities'. 'You tell these stories for so long that they seem true,' she confessed. 'Nothing that boy did could ever justify what happened to him.'

I am writing this in a small cottage on a farm in Suffolk. The main room houses a collection devoted to the American Civil Rights Movement; above my desk is a photograph of the Tallahatchie River next to a long shelf of books on Emmett Till. Three months after his death, Rosa Parks, haunted by Till's murder, refused to give up her seat on a bus in Montgomery, Alabama. Her arrest sparked a bus boycott that brought a young minister called Martin Luther King Jr into the movement.

The latest volume added to my collection is *The Blood of Emmett Till*, the book that contains Mrs Bryant's confession. It is one of the gravest 'post truths' in American history. I only wish the writer had revealed it 10 years earlier. There's no guarantee the revelation would have reduced the venom of hate that still stalks America's political landscape, but it might, just might, make us all wary of fake news and post truths which are really only lies.

May 3, 2017

MODERATE, WITH FOG PATCHES

IN idle moments, I like to think of titles. Once, lost in the poetry of the *Shipping Forecast* while driving to Lincoln when it was my husband's constituency, I thought of a title for his political memoir: *Moderate, With Fog Patches*. This slim volume is yet to be written.

I was born in a small town called Greenwood, but a much-loved great-aunt lived a few miles away in a two-stoplight town called Itta Bena. My departure from the South was a journey lit up by the crosses of the Ku Klux Klan. It was a scary and unhappy time, but my life has turned out to be better than I ever could have expected. It's given me a title for my own unwritten memoir: *Don't Cry For Me, Itta Bena*.

I do like the chomp of a good title. A few have had the potent comfort of prayer beads, steadying me and pushing me forward. *I Would Have Saved Them If I Could* has pulled me out of the quicksand of lost time for nearly four decades. The title of the collection of short stories by Leonard Michaels, it's been a valuable warning: sometimes you cannot save the alcoholic friend/the brilliant chef with the destructive temper/ the couple at one another's throats/the girlfriend who goes from one crazy man to another.

It's like an invisible tattoo that reminds me that I am not a heart surgeon, a psychoanalyst, a faith healer or a life coach. I'm a patient listener and, I like to think, dispenser of wise advice, and I would save them if I could but sometimes I just can't. (I've passed it on to friends whose lives were stuck in the delusion of salvation, explaining that it's the title of a story about the marriage of the writer's parents. When I Googled the story just now, I read it was about the Holocaust. Good lord. How did I miss that? I'm not sure I'll ever see the title in the same way again.)

Another title that flashes in my head a lot these days is Grace Paley's *Enormous Changes at the Last Minute*. Change, even enormous change, comes in many sizes. A grave diagnosis makes you see your life in a whole new light. And, a month later, a reprieve: it wasn't that, it was this and easily treated with a single course of antibiotics. In no time, you go back to who you were before.

Although we still wake up each morning, turn on the radio and make the coffee, who could have predicted that the world – our own world – would become a battlefield for ISIS? Back in 1993, a friend visiting from California brought me a long article by the academic Samuel Huntington called *The Clash of Civilizations*. In it, the writer predicted a post-Cold War new world order shaped not by a clash of countries but of cultures. He warned that Islamic extremism would be the biggest threat to world peace. Although a man of great intelligence, I thought Huntington's predictions sounded Old Testament. The title now causes me to tremble when I think of it.

These days, life feels plagued by too many changes at the last minute. No one I know, Leavers or Remainers, really believed that Brexit was coming round the mountain. And when it did, no one believed that David Cameron wouldn't hang in there, however miserable or ridiculous he felt. It's all change, but so far, so vague. Nobody can say what Brexit really means.

However, Brexit feels like bite-size change compared with the property and casino developer who is now President of the USA. The enormity of that change at the last minute still has hearts pounding and heads shaking around the world.

Farmers don't like enormous changes, long-term or last-minute. Routine is our fertiliser of choice. Our idea of adventure and derring-do is gliding across wheat fields in a John Deere combine during harvest when there's a full moon. When your livelihood depends more on the weather than on sensible endeavour, that's all the uncertainty you can handle. Last month, we lost 80% of the grape harvest in back-to-back frosts. Those grapes – and the wheat, the barley, the sugar beet and potatoes – are my bid for security.

The world is pretty shaky right now and, for better or for worse, security is what most people want, whether they till the soil or sing the blues for a living.

By the time these words acquire the dubious significance that comes from appearing in print, the General Election will be hours away. I'm a conscientious voter, inspired by another good title, Delmore Schwartz's story called *In Dreams Begin Responsibilities*. (He got the title from W. B. Yeats, who borrowed it from an unidentified 'old play'.) I confess that I feel nervous.

Every election now feels like a Catch-22, a title that has passed into the language as a description of the impossible bind. Voters aren't entirely convinced by one candidate, but have a dread of the other candidate, who promises enormous change. Actually, even Joseph Heller's title was changed at the last minute, after Leon Uris published *Mila 18* just months before Heller's book, originally called *Catch-18*, was delivered to the printers.

Sometimes great titles are just luck. The writer Margaret Mitchell was asked to come up with a new list because her publisher wasn't crazy about a big novel called *Tomorrow is Another Day*. Under pressure, she came up with *Gone With the Wind*. The truth is, enlightenment requires more than a title. We are living in chaotic and complicated times, and we could all use a period of calm. There is much to be said for Moderate. Even with fog patches.

June 7, 2017

LOOKING FOR GLADNESS
IN THESE TIMES

LET me start with the good news. The spotted flycatchers are back. These hard-working migrants have flown all the way from Africa, and, night and day, they dart about with the speed and grace of stagehands shifting scenery. Thanks to their determination, we've had a summer free of fly swatters and sticky strips covered in flies. If the gift of citizenship was in my hands, it would be theirs.

More good news: rain. Two weeks ago, we had what Delta farmers call 'a million-dollar rain'. Before, the crops resembled flotsam on a beach. After three days of gentle rain, the sugar beet and potatoes met in the rows and the wheat and barley had backbone. Farm prices being what they are, it's more like a 'ten bucks' rain, but it's better than a shoeshine.

Another blessing: roses. The garden has been as lavish as a homecoming parade. I'm a believer in old-fashioned, sweet-smelling varieties – what my grandmother called 'High Church' roses. These one-bloom-only varieties give me an excuse to stay put so I don't miss their brief appearance and the felicity of summer evenings drinking wine in the company of Fantin-Latour and Mme Alfred Carrière.

The garden has had another, unexpected, role. It's been a refuge, a patch of guilty peace during this summer of our discontent. Three terrorist attacks, an election nobody wanted that ended with a wheel falling off a wagon that was heading who knows where and, looming over London, the Grenfell Tower is now a blackened mausoleum, emblem of a tragedy that affects everyone who claims a beating heart. In East Anglia, the sky is empty save for church towers and grain stores. We can't imagine what it's like to be told: 'You are not safe. Leave your home.' Each morning, we greet each other with the same question: what's next?

My constant companion, in good times and bad, is the radio, but in this uneasy season it's provided little comfort. *Farming Today* tells the early riser of record dolphin deaths from fishing nets, and warns that the 80,000 farm workers who pick and pack the nation's summer fruit and salads are put off by the Brexit message and the pound being worth 20% less than last year.

Then, *Today*. Don't the presenters know the news is sad enough without their pushing and shoving? However many times I say 'Down, Nick!' or 'Stop it, John!', nobody gets the message: you can't bully the truth out of folks.

In the afternoon, I shell broad beans in the

courteous company of Matthew Bannister on *Last Word*, the obituaries programme. In a summer when so many anonymous people have died, I compose a letter in my head: 'Dear Mr Bannister, May I request an alternative *Last Word*? No one we've ever heard of, just names we should know: the young Italian architect Gloria Trevisan, who was about to start conservation work on Wren's Royal Hospital, and her partner, Marco Gottardi, an assistant at the Anglo-Italian practice CIAO. The young couple were excited about living at the top of a tower with its views of London. And could you include the two soldiers who died in a tank explosion. Corporals Matthew 'Hattie' Hatfield and Darren 'Daz' Neilson, both fathers of two-year-old daughters...

I'm still mulling over my letter when Mr Bannister says that the last words on *Last Word* will be a poem by Helen Dunmore, the writer who died of cancer, aged 64. I expect to hear the poem she wrote in the last week of her life, but it's an earlier one, *Glad of These Times*:

> Driving along the motorway
> Swerving the packed lanes
> I am glad of these times.
> Because I did not die in childbirth
> Because my children will survive me
> I am glad of these times.

Glad of these times? When did you last say that?

What I say, what all my friends of a certain age guiltily admit, is that we have lived in the best of times and we've been careless with our legacy. Dunmore names things that give her gladness: she is not hungry; she can lock her door with her own key; she is the beneficiary of central heating, email, keyhole surgery, polio inoculations and cashback, of power showers and 20 types of yoghurt.

In her honour, I begin a list of my own. I start small – the broad beans in my lap; Silver Queen corn ripening in the fields; sweet peas; a kitchen in which I can sit, chop, peel, read and listen; a blue bowl that has held the home-grown tomatoes of three generations of women. I'm glad for the three Jamaican midwives at Hammersmith Hospital who were strong and kind when I felt neither, and who were guests of honour at Sam's christening. For a husband whose Englishness has endowed him with a knowledge of wild flowers and a passion for John Buchan, cricket and devilled kidneys that I've never shared. I'm glad he tolerates the things that fill me with gladness: peacocks, chickens, turkeys, the recordings of Janet Baker, Kathleen Ferrier, Glenn Gould and Elvis played on a loop.

Because I possess a much newer British passport than citizens born here, I have a fiercer, more territorial sense of Britishness. I'm not glad that Qatar Holdings owns the British jewels – The Connaught, Claridge's, The Berkeley, Harrods, 95% of The Shard, 50% of Canary Wharf, one side of

Grosvenor Square (the former American Embassy), the Olympic Village – and is building a mega-palace out of three houses in Regent's Park. I'm not glad that the white stucco homes of leafy London streets are unoccupied, bought with funds from Russia, Hong Kong and Saudi Arabia.

I know, I know: one minute I sound like the *Daily Mail*, the next like Jeremy Corbyn, but I want Britain to reclaim its heart and soul and neighbourhoods. I know no one who wants Hinkley Point built by the French and the Chinese. How did we reach this strange disjunction in which we speak of sovereignty and sell the deeds to the highest bidder? What do we have to do before we can write 'glad of these times'?

We are an old country that has moved with the times, but never abandoned the past. The monarchy is proof of that: from Elizabeth I to Elizabeth II, there have been bumpy times, but 'steadfast' and 'survival' stand out. When The Queen begins her Birthday Message with, 'It is difficult to escape a very sombre national mood', we are reminded that her presence humanises and unifies us, whether we know it or not.

Many things give us a sense of who we are. We like black taxis, red buses, *Antiques Roadshow*, *Bake Off*, *Foyle's War*, English apples, Irish sweaters, Scotch whisky, Welsh singing. We're proud that Harry Potter is English, but relieved that Scottish independence has hit a lull. We're amazed that *Downton Abbey* is as famous as Big Ben. We lip-sync Churchill's speeches, get married to the vows in the Book of Common Prayer, and hope to go to our grave with the same perfect, powerful language, aided by Auden and Larkin, Shakespeare and Rossetti. The murdered MP Jo Cox got it right when she said in her maiden speech that we have more in common than things that divide us, and it begins with our common language.

John Donne wrote 'no man is an island', but it turns out that even an island isn't an island. The world beyond is in turmoil, and, like the butterfly that flaps its wings a continent away, we feel every tremor. And yet, despite a season of chaos, ours is a complex history of compassion, sacrifice, courage and kindness. What we choose to emphasise in our history determines our capacity to repair, to heal and to create a more equal land.

I once saw the words of the poet Alasdair Gray painted on the walls of a converted church in Glasgow: 'Work as if you live in the early days of a better nation.' If we heed the advice of poets, I believe the time will come when we can say with a clear conscience: 'We are glad of these times.'

July 5, 2017

MOVING WITH THE TIMES

THE invitation did not say 'End of an Era' or 'Passing the Torch', but everyone seemed to know it was. Driving through the 400-acre deer park with its ancient oaks, walking across the bridge over the deep moat and into the courtyard, it was as much a personal story as a journey through English history. This was a Suffolk gathering with the collective memory of another party held here a decade earlier.

That was a gala evening celebrating the unbroken residency of the same family in this house for 500 years. The night ended with fireworks reflected in the moat and accompanied by music, a stupendous spectacle made possible by speakers in the park the size of freight cars.

Our generous hosts, still stylish, beautiful and youthful, brought this house and estate into the 21st century with taste, originality and social conscience. Now, they're moving out of the grand manor house and into the smaller house on the estate where they began their married life in 1970. Their eldest son and his young family are moving in.

If you check volume 1 A–M of the *Shorter Oxford English Dictionary*, first published in 1933 and reprinted with corrections in 1959, the word 'downsizing' does not appear. What happened in novels as well as in real life was the unwritten tribal procedure of aristocratic primogeniture: the husband died and his widow moved into the dower house. If there was no dower house, she might be persuaded to move into another house on the estate.

Failing that, a flat near Peter Jones. In Vita Sackville-West's *All Passion Spent*, the 85-year-old widowed Lady Slane buys a small cottage in remote Hampstead, a move so daring that it shocks her friends and children.

Times have changed. The dower house may have been sold when Inheritance Tax was 98%, lost after the debacle with Lloyd's of London or because too many generations have lived off the capital. More significantly, we now live in the age of titanium hips, triple bypasses, stents, statins, flu shots, pneumonia shots and airbags. We haven't yet conquered the Grim Reaper, but we have triumphed over at least one of Man's initial handicaps: the brevity of life.

Despite the alarm bells in medical columns, we are living longer, and, if each generation stays put in the 'Big House' until death does one part, the next generation can't bring the sunlight, oxygen, fun and sheer stamina needed to keep these demanding big houses and estates alive. The wise and the brave recognise this and plan their departure while they have the energy and imagination to embark on the new passage.

There is a palpable sense of excitement in couples who make the move. It's as if the decades of stewardship – bringing life to the garden, converting the stables into a wedding venue and the old smithy into tea rooms, organising garden festivals, music festivals, farm shops – have been an exciting and complicated meal. Moving out – and creating their new, smaller house in which ancestral portraits and dark furniture are replaced with modern pictures, pale sofas and *tout confort* – this is the lovely dessert.

Even without the moated house and 5,000 acres, the urge to downsize before it's forced upon you by sickness, old age or the death of a spouse is a powerful one. Reading in the *FT Weekend* about wine writer Jancis Robinson and her husband, Nicholas Lander, selling their four-storey Victorian house in Belsize Park and moving into a large top-floor apartment in King's Cross could fill the most dedicated lover of country life with envy. Even the descriptions about spending 'every free weekend for more than a year throwing things out', giving away the piano, culling and recycling until the last day, feel like a tale of courage and deliverance.

On a more modest level, it's what more and

more country folk are doing – moving out of their patch of rural paradise where life depends on the car. All around me, couples whose children have left home are now moving into their nearest market town. They miss the chickens and the kitchen garden, but they brag about being able to walk to the cinema, restaurants, shops, train station and GP. They celebrate the freedom and independence that 'downsizing' provides. They may not walk home after a movie followed by risotto and a glass of Sauvignon Blanc at Carluccio's every night, but they like knowing that they can.

Leaving the ancient moated manor house on a large estate is a little more complicated. It requires timing and preparation comparable to putting on the Olympics. It also requires a son or daughter, not necessarily the eldest, who is up for the role and has what it takes to hold it all together. Sometimes that isn't obvious, even to the hopeful parents, but the belief that generation must tread upon the heels of generation is a law of nature embedded in our DNA. The history of this country indicates that its landed aristocracy has survived this long because of its capacity to make the 'leap of faith'.

As for the couple giving the party, their family motto bodes well: *Confido Conquiesco* – I trust and am content.

August 2, 2017

THE MYTH OF THE LOST CAUSE

ALTHOUGH the roots of this English estate go back to Domesday, the garden at Wyken has a Southern accent, as in Deep South. The iron gate leading to the kitchen garden is made of cornstalks entwined with morning glory, cast from the same mouldings that created the famous railings surrounding the Cornstalk House in New Orleans. I found the originals here in England, bought six panels and welded them together.

Then there's the Red Hot Border. My Mississippi grandmother believed every garden needed something 'a little *vulgah*'. She reckoned that if you stick to pale pinks and creamy magnolias you end up with a garden for sleepwalkers. She shared Nancy Lancaster's belief that white furniture looks like aspirin in the garden, which is why the first thing you see when you arrive are five rocking chairs painted a dusky blue-grey. I wouldn't go so far as to call it 'Confederate Grey', but Miss Lancaster and her Virginia-born aunt, Nancy Astor, wouldn't have flinched at describing it as that.

I hardly notice what else is Southern in this Suffolk

manor house, but as I watched the hell that unfolded in Charlottesville three weeks ago things began to stick out. On the Elizabethan table in the hall is a leather-bound shooting script of *Gone With the Wind*. It was left to me by Will Price, the voice coach who taught Vivien Leigh and Leslie Howard their Southern accents. Most Americans never knew that Scarlett and Ashley were actually English. It's inscribed: 'For Will Price who literally shoved the South down our throats. With good wishes always, David Selznick.'

Something else that I found in a box of my grandmother's letters: a carved figure no taller than my thumb that stands in the window above the kitchen sink. He's not handsome or dignified – his head is almost as large as his body – but it captures his fine profile. It's Robert E. Lee, and his aristocratic nose was always his best feature.

I've often thought about removing Lee from my kitchen, but he got a reprieve after I saw the movie *Lincoln*. In the last scene the war finally ended, with 620,000 dead. As the defeated general, his face old with sadness, arrives on his bony horse Traveller and, with the slight lifting of his hat, surrenders to Gen. Grant at Appomattox, I began to weep.

Days later, I remembered Lee's most quoted words: 'It is well that war is so terrible, or we should grow too fond of it.' And the words of Tacitus that Shelby Foote borrowed for his final volume of *The Civil War*: 'They make a wilderness and call it peace.'

The forlorn Lee was a crucial image in my early education. We were brought up with the 'Lost Cause' version of a war that was always called 'The War Between the States'. When I was a yellow-headed lap baby, my great-aunts told me that my belly button was 'where the Yankee shot you'. By the time I could read, I knew the Civil War was a tragedy, that Reconstruction was a cruel, unjust and prolonged punishment of the South and that Lee was an honourable, brave gentleman, a soldier so distinguished that Lincoln asked him to lead the Union troops. His choosing the Confederacy over the Union is one of the most famous decisions in American history.

We were never taught that the war was about the human bondage of slavery. We were taught that the South fought it for a more worldly cause: to vindicate State Sovereignty, a war of Northern aggression against Southern constitutional rights.

I ended up leaving the South in the 1960s, freed by my emancipated view of race and humanity. However, the moral high ground is a slippery slope: I didn't understand that the myths you learn in childhood reside in the blood like dormant viruses. Old memories returned as I watched the news from Virginia and the civilised, beautiful city of Charlottesville. I looked at the white faces illuminated by torches, chanting the vile anti-Semitic rants of the 1930s, the neo-Nazis and Klansmen. A century and a half later, after the war that forms the most traumatic scar in its young history, America is still a divided nation engaged in a battle for its soul.

Few historians think Lee is a good symbol for white supremacists. Yes, he was a slaveholder – so was Grant – but Lee was a complex man who called slavery 'a moral and political evil'. He hated the idea of erecting monuments to Confederate soldiers, writing: 'I think it wiser not to keep open the sores of war but to follow the examples of those nations who endeavoured to obliterate the marks of civil strife. To commit to oblivion the feelings engendered.'

My miniature Lee now rests in a shoebox in the attic on a bed of 1,000 Confederate dollars that lost their value long before that war ended. I think that Lee would also be relieved to vacate the square in Charlottesville and find peace in a museum dedicated to telling both sides of the saddest story in America's history.

If you want to remember the man, there is a monument that will last as long as America endures. Called Arlington National Cemetery, 'the nation's most hallowed ground', it was Lee's family estate. Seized by the US Government early in the war, it became the burial ground for the Union dead. It is now the resting place of American soldiers of every race and creed, a piece of land where the furies of civil strife are finally committed to oblivion.

September 6, 2017

71

BASE IS THE SLAVE THAT PAYS

NEARLY 20 years ago I wrote a column for *Country Life* inspired by Nick Hornby's novel *About a Boy*. Will, a smug consumer aesthete, fills out a magazine questionnaire in search of the 'cool' profile of its readers. Will is 'Ultra Cool': he's slept with a woman he hardly knew (5 points), spent more than £300 on a jacket (5 points) and eaten at a restaurant that serves polenta and shaved Parmesan (3 points).

The questionnaire prompted my own cool inventory. Despite a horizon of wheat fields, far from Will's edgy world, I felt pretty cool. Heck, I owned a restaurant that served polenta with shaved Parmesan (5 points), although my customers prefer potatoes (deduct 10 points).

Reading it now, Will doesn't sound so cool. In two decades we have created a digital universe that makes his world seem as quaint as *Antiques Roadshow*. I wrote that column on an Apricot word processor and faxed it to *Country Life*. I'm writing this column on an Apple laptop, my fourth Apple computer. I have an Apple iPhone (my third phone, my second iPhone) and a 12-year-old iPad. All this Apple stuff would have got me lots of cool points when being an Apple person made you a member of the counter-culture. Now, more people have iPhones than toothbrushes, and the citizens of the world are spellbound by their small screen. The only element of counter-culture is Apple's, which cunningly registers its headquarters in low-tax countries (Ireland: corporate tax rate 12.5%) and pays miniscule tax (UK: 19%) in the country where its gargantuan profits are made. But, hey, thanks to Apple and iPhones, we have Airbnb!

I stayed in an Airbnb (5 points) in Copenhagen found by my son and daughter-in-law. I kept quiet about the half-empty shampoo bottles in the shower, the clean but un-ironed sheets and the pillows that had shared many heads before mine. Instead, I dwelt on how authentic it felt to be in a capital city in a real neighbourhood (5 points). This was two years before Airbnb began to take over city centres, with landlords buying up flats, filling them with IKEA furniture and avoiding those pesky health-and-safety regulations imposed on B&Bs and hotels.

London now has 40,000 listings on the site, and Airbnb has come a long way from the days of the micro-entrepreneur sharing a flat for the weekend. It's also deprived the market of valuable property regulated for short-let properties. Like Apple, Airbnb's profits generated from the UK are not taxed here, but in Ireland, as are its profits from Paris and Amsterdam.

Then there is Uber. I admit I've made many Uber journeys with my son who, like most twenty-somethings, has an account. There have been times when, searching for a black cab, I've been grateful for him reaching for his iPhone and an Uber arriving in minutes. In Copenhagen, we went everywhere by Uber. It felt like magic.

Problem is, it doesn't feel so cool when you learn that there are now 40,000 Uber drivers licensed in London, clogging the streets there and in villages near Heathrow and Stansted, where they wait for calls from passengers walking into arrivals. Or that each Uber driver is listed as a separate business, which means Uber is not liable to pay VAT and the drivers receive no benefits. Passengers pay fares directly to the driver, who automatically hands over a commission fee that appears in the company's Dutch accounts. In 2016, Uber's turnover in the UK was more than £23 million. It paid tax of £411,000.

Shall I go on? I remember thinking that Amazon was a miraculous gift to country folk. I was euphoric as I greedily ordered books and videos at midnight. Then, my favourite mail-order book company, A Common Reader, went out of business. Much-loved bookshops disappeared. A favourite country-clothing shop shut. You could count the empty shop fronts in market towns – shops that paid rents and rates and employed staff, but couldn't compete with Amazon. The price we pay for cheap and fast is high indeed, Amazon's not so much: a £37 million tax bill on sales of £7 billion in 2016.

How do I know all these figures? I Googled them, of course. Good old Google, life raft of the baby boomers with fading memories. Can't remember which character in Shakespeare says 'Base is the slave that pays'? Google it! Want to get to Avignon by train? Google it! But don't Google Google's tax payments in the UK because it will depress you.

Nobody wants to think that all the cool things that make our lives easier have backfired and have become like Frankenstein's monster. We're wired to believe that easier, faster and cheaper is wonderful, not that it exploits workers and erodes the tax base that pays for life-saving healthcare, education, public transport and good roads – things more important than iPhones and discount books.

Even when our democratic institutions are threatened (that means you, Facebook), and Twitter in the wrong hands could trigger a war, our outrage is hazy. These monsters can't be put back in the cauldron because now we can't imagine life without them. They also can't live without us, which means we have to match their highly paid lawyers and accountants and make companies pay tax in the country where they make their big bucks. We should regulate them as fiercely as they regulate us.

PS: It's Pistol in *Henry V* who says 'Base is the slave that pays'. Thanks for that, Google, but I don't think it's a cool company motto. Deduct 5 points.

October 4, 2017

TO ENDURE AND PREVAIL

THE writer Garrison Keillor has announced that he's off lingonberries, Volvos and flatpack white furniture from IKEA. Even the meatballs are off the menu. America's big-hearted writer is on a Swedish no-go because he's had it with the humourless Swedes who have given yet another Nobel prize to a writer whose contribution to literature is incomprehensible, pretentious and bleak. His only consolation: 'At least they didn't give it to Joni Mitchell.'

I think that's pretty hard on Kazuo Ishiguro. When I heard on *Today* that he'd won, I felt a wave of happiness. Not because I've read all his books, but because he's a British writer and I thought: 'A triumph for the English language!' My husband's response was more prosaic. 'Who is this Ishiguro? He doesn't sound English.'

He was even more mystified by the Nobel committee's praise of the Japanese-born English Ishiguro as a writer who 'has uncovered the abyss beneath our illusory sense of connection with the world'. 'What on earth does that mean?' he asked.

I am married to an Englishman who believes that the high calling of literature is to lead people *out* of the abyss. I've never wandered to my desk without hearing his wistful plea: 'Try to make people feel better.' Although Mr Keillor and I share politics, music and poetry (I begin every morning with him on www.writersalmanac. com), I didn't give up my Volvo just because the Swedes reward hard and often dreary writers. I come from the poorest state in the Union, and our greatest source of pride was we had a Nobel Prize winner.

Admittedly, when William Faulkner won in 1949 no more than 10 people in the state of Mississippi had read a word he'd written. He was deep in debt and out of print everywhere except in France, a country that believes pretentious and incomprehensible rhymes with intellectual. But, for nearly seven decades, Mississippians have been grateful that Faulkner's prize hitched their mule and wagon to the wider world and showed that, along with cotton, catfish, imbeciles, ringworm and lynching, we were a land of storytellers. Without that Nobel Prize, I reckon Mr Faulkner would still be out of print.

When Nobel created his legacy in 1896, he wanted it to go to the writer of 'the most outstanding work in an ideal direction'. His family fought the provision in his will, so the awards were stalled until 1901, when the first prize went to French poet and essayist Sully Prudhomme.

The names of Nobel Laureates whose workshop is the English language – Rudyard Kipling, who, at 41, is still the youngest ever winner, Yeats, Shaw, Eliot, Churchill, Hemingway, Beckett, Golding, Heaney, Pinter, Lessing, V. S. Naipaul, Alice Munro and last year's surprise winner Bob Dylan – reads like a roll call of writers who have put their heart and soul into the written word.

Britain's newest literary Nobel Laureate, known as Ish by friends, is a worthy member of the club. He was born in Nagasaki in 1954; his mother, still alive and very proud of her son, survived the atomic bomb. His father, an oceanographer, moved the family to England in 1959 and settled in Surrey. The family planned to go back to Japan someday, but, when Ish was 15, they decided to stay in England. In 1983, aged 29, he became a British citizen.

If you're born nine years after the atom bomb has levelled the city of your birth, you could be forgiven if some existential darkness seeps into your writing. Faulkner's most famous quote, 'The past is never dead, It's not even past', often omits the next line: 'All of us labour in webs spun long before we were born.' If ever a writer was destined to labour in those webs, surely it was Ishiguro. The first two of his eight novels are set in Nagasaki as the city was struggling to recover.

Restless times back then. Restless times now. Scenes of floods, forest fires, terrorist attacks, ancient cities reduced to rubble, millions in refugee camps, worldwide debt and two unpredictable men with the deadliest weapons known to mankind at their fingertips. It would take a partially deaf writing genius to sidestep this man-made abyss.

When Faulkner accepted his prize in Stockholm in 1950, he was painfully aware that the bombs that had fallen five years earlier had replaced the artists' concerns of the spirit with the basest fear: 'When will I be blown up?' Faulkner, however, urged the writer to fight against his fear, that it's the writer's 'privilege to help man endure by lifting his heart, by reminding him of the courage and honour and hope and pride and compassion and pity and sacrifice'. He believed that the writer's voice should be one of the pillars 'to help him endure and prevail'.

And now I'm worried that I haven't made you feel better. Go and buy Faulkner's *The Sound and the Fury* and Mr Ishiguro's *A Pale View of Hills*, his first novel about a Japanese family coming to live in England. Three continents, two Nobel Prize winners, one great language and worth the journey.

Put a log on the fire. Join Mr Keillor on The Writer's Almanac. Serve meatballs with lingonberries – they go together like readers and writers. And say a quiet prayer of gratitude for a prize that ensures writers like Faulkner and Mr Ishiguro will prevail and readers will endure.

November 1, 2017

LIFE ON THE SILVER MOUNTAIN

'TIS the season when it's better to give than receive. That sounds good to me because I'm a woman who has lived an acquisitive life and has now reached the giving stage. And, truly, I have a lot of stuff to give.

For a start, I'm sitting on a silver mine. As the last granddaughter to marry, I inherited my grandmother's and my mother's silver (a total of 24 place settings). My married sister and the female cousinage all had their own hoard of 'wedding silver': an ornate pattern called Francis the 1st that Southern girls choose long before they meet the man they will marry.

I managed to survive more than three decades without a silver pattern or a husband, but when I finally said 'I do' I was rewarded with a silver haul of two generations at once.

For 30 years, nestled in its soft, dove-grey livery marked 'Hagerty', it's lain in the gun safe because I married a man with his own significant pile of family silver: dining room (with the little lion silver mark) and kitchen (silver plate, no lion). I embraced his hefty silver, crest and all, and added Southern expertise: polish your silver at least three days before you use it because the smell of polish lingers. Rinse well in hot water, and dry immediately with a soft cloth. Never use a silver dip. Toothbrushes are not allowed on intricate pieces, but badger shaving brushes are.

Once, silver meant value and security. We knew the fields where it was buried in the Civil War so the Yankees wouldn't find it, in cocoons of old quilts and flour sacks (not wool because lanolin corrodes). Even now, no Southern woman in her right mind would wrap silver in newspaper or clingfilm. We are born knowing that.

For more than a quarter century I muddled along in my contented silvery state. Then, a beloved Danish friend left me his Georg Jensen Acorn pattern service for 12, but with pieces that might mystify even Carson at *Downton Abbey*, including eight spoon sizes: tea, demitasse, mocha, dessert, soup, ice tea, ice cream and dinner. Beautiful, but a spoonful too far.

In an act of familial loyalty, I called my cousin Jamie in California (Francis the 1st), who has three married sons. 'Would any of your boys – well, their wives – want our grandmother's silver?' A long silence. 'My daughters-in-law watch my silver ceremony each holiday – the unwrapping, polishing, hand washing – and think I'm nuts. It's just not how they live.'

Next, I called my sister (ditto, Francis the 1st): 'Lord, no! My sons aren't interested. I'm ready to sell it all and spend the money on winter vacations somewhere warm.'

Passing silver to family feels ancestral; selling it feels like sacrilege, but that chain is broken. Go on to eBay or 1stDibs and there are so many sets of Acorn that you realise you've left it too late. The silver-canteen mountain has appeared as one generation downsizes and the next says: 'Simplify. Dishwasher only.' Add to that the walnut desk, the French *armoire*, the mahogany table and 12 Georgian chairs with genuine black horsehair upholstery, the satinwood *demi-lunes*. Our heirs don't have room, and they don't want them.

Guess what? Christie's, Sotheby's, Bonhams and Phillips don't either. Regional salerooms are more diplomatic and accepting, but don't book Christmas in the Seychelles based on your Welsh dresser and oak gate-leg table: you'll be lucky to get the train fare to Hastings.

As antique shops have disappeared, so have second-hand bookshops. The day when dealers gazed appreciatively at your shelves and wrote a nice cheque are over: your books are only worth the pleasure they give you. Unless you have rare first editions inscribed by the author, they are not an investment. Ditto, most of the pictures on your walls.

Unless you live at Chatsworth, your chattels are unlikely to be a nest egg for you or your descendants. 'Lasting value' is a mythological creature with foreign-sounding name because the planet is crowded and our streets and houses are crowded. It's the Age of Too Much Stuff, thanks to cheaper goods, cheaper shipping and greater prosperity. Even the charity shops are flooded with too much stuff.

I usually begin December with a pleasurable wander through the house, choosing books, china, quilts and, yes, silver – treasures to bestow on 'the young'. Yesterday, my treasures were waiting to be wrapped when I paused for a coffee and picked up *Letters from Klara*, a new translation of short stories by Tove Jansson, written in her seventies.

In the title story, Klara, elderly yet acute, writes to her friend: 'I assume you're getting rid of stuff, a perfectly natural and commendable activity. I've been doing it myself and have gradually learned a thing or two. One of them is that the little treasures you try to give young people just make them uncomfortable – more and more polite and more and more uncomfortable.'

Think of what that means. It means we need to accept that 'value', like people, has a finite lifespan, that 'choice' is more valuable than 'stuff', and that even the old truths evolve. Crystal, china or silver no longer have to be the gift that goes on giving.

December 6, 2017

III
The Melody At Night

THE WORLD OUR WILDERNESS

I LIKE the word 'lacuna'. It's one of those words that sounds like one thing – an exotic South American animal, a rare moth – and means another: 'unfilled gap or space'. This confusion has left the word under-used, but I rely on it each year between Christmas and New Year. 'Oh, welcome lacuna!' I say when the Christmas frenzy is over and the aimless peace of leftovers descends.

Nobody in my household admires this linguistic beauty mark, which doesn't bother me because I like to begin the new year in bed. My idea of bliss is to wander downstairs, let the dog out, make a cup of coffee, feed the dog and go back to bed with my coffee. The writer Rose Macaulay got it right: 'Only one hour in the normal day is more pleasurable than the hour spent in bed with a book before going to sleep and that is the hour spent in bed with a book after being called in the morning.'

Dear Rose. Whatever happened to her? A Dame of the British Empire and a writer who published 36 books, including a chatty one on Milton and 23 novels, plus poetry and essays, letters and travel pieces, and is now unread.

I discovered her on a pilgrimage to Grantchester in Cambridgeshire. As I gazed at the Old Vicarage, a Margaret Rutherford lookalike next to me snapped: 'He stole it!' 'Stole it?' 'Stole the words! "And is there honey still for tea?" was Rose Macaulay's. It's in her novel *The Valley Captives*. Published in 1911. And I bet you've never heard of her!'

In fact, I'd come across the name in letters and diaries of other writers – Virginia Woolf, V. S. Pritchett, Penelope Fitzgerald – and I told the story of this encounter for years but never made the effort to find out if it was true. Then I came across the novel in an Oxfam bookshop and there it was: a tortured young man who looks back on his country childhood as a haven of bees and honey and wonders: 'And will there be honey for tea?'

I'm willing to forgive Rupert Brooke, despite the irony that it's his most famous line and Macaulay has vanished from all but the dustiest of shelves. But who knows? Perhaps she pinched the line from Brooke when they went swimming – they were friends, he was a pupil of her father's, he introduced her to literary London. If the tumultuous days of 2017, with its Fake News, alternative facts and accusations and convictions without trial have taught us anything, it's to be wary of the first version of anything.

At the heart of our new Orwellian age is something more troubling than doublespeak and false truth: it's that we all believe *only what we want to believe*. I plead guilty. I genuinely believe that the recent Republican candidate for senator in Alabama chased underage girls when he was in his thirties, but I don't believe that Garrison Keillor, a writer on my side of the political divide, is guilty of anything that could merit being sacked from his radio programme, although in neither case do I have access to the facts (call it evidence).

I believe and disbelieve these things, not to keep believing nimble but the opposite: to reinforce the concrete structure of my thinking. It's why I'd never watch Fox News, but am faithful as a nun to the BBC's *Beyond 100 Days* with Katty Kay and Christian Fraser, because I detect a mutual scepticism, a similar funny bone, a shared political astonishment.

I may be up and down about Brexit, vacillating about Hard or Soft Exit and wavering about Theresa May, but I have no time for Jean-Claude Juncker, Donald Tusk and Michel Barnier, who behave like a confederacy of jilted partners, determined to cause as much misery and extract as much alimony as they can. In the same vein, if I read tomorrow that Boris Johnson dived into the North Sea to save a drowning dog, he wouldn't get my vote. I'd be pretty sure he wrote the story.

I'm not proud of sounding like the 100-year-old

woman 'who died with all her own prejudices'. It's a terrible way to live, entrenched under our tribal laws – Red states versus Blue states, Israel versus Palestine, Conservative versus Labour, Anglo-Catholics versus Evangelicals, climate changers versus climate deniers. We're now united only in making civilisation less civilised every day.

It's all the more reason to go back to bed with the dog, mug of coffee and good book. This lacuna will end all too soon. In a few days we begin pruning the vines, an act of faith. A team of builders will arrive to take down the old grain store built in the 1950s, sided in asbestos. That was another act of faith. The clean pages of my new diary will soon be blurred with appointments, meetings, deadlines.

Bed beckons. In case you're wondering, the book is Macaulay's *The World My Wilderness*. It's her best known, although the writer Sybille Bedford preferred *Crewe Train*. She liked the description of the publisher, who 'felt about books as doctors feel about medicine, or managers about plays – cynical but hopeful'. Cynical but hopeful: three better words to ease one into the new year I know not.

January 3, 2018

COUNTING OUT LOUD

ALTHOUGH I had to repeat Algebra I and II at school, and the puzzles on *Today* are as mystifying to me as Aramaic, I have a deep respect for numbers. I can ponder for days over statistics released by the Centers for Disease Control and Prevention (CDC) in Atlanta, Georgia. For instance: more than 40,000 Americans died in car accidents in 2016. I found that astonishing, but more shocking still is that more than half were not wearing seatbelts.

For years, road accidents have been the single largest cause of death in the USA. No longer: it's now drug overdoses. In 2016, there were more than 64,000 deaths and, of those, more than 20,000 were related to 'synthetic opioids'. This means that in one year more Americans died of drug overdoses than died in the war in Vietnam (58,200) during a 20-year period.

The opioid plague is putting gun deaths in a new light. According to the CDC, in 2016 there were more than 38,000 gun-related deaths in the USA, 4,000 up on 2015. Two-thirds were suicides, but 11,000 were homicides. After the mass shooting at the First Baptist Church of Sutherland Springs, Texas, last year, the President said it was prompted by a 'mental-health issue' and wasn't about guns. I don't have mental-health statistics, but, according to Wikipedia, Congress has prohibited the CDC from conducting research that advocates in favour of gun control. The CDC has interpreted this ban to extend to all research on gun-violence prevention, and hasn't funded any research on the subject since 1996.

By now, you're probably thinking this column is about as cheerful as *Three Billboards Outside Ebbing, Missouri*. Here are some happier numbers: Bitcoin has gone down in value! True, the cyber-currency is still up 900% in a year, so losing $3,000 in a day doesn't mean much, but, as it's unlikely that you or I have any, we don't have to feel bad about missing the boat – or not knowing what Bitcoin is.

More good statistics: concern over Brexit has brought down the price of farmland in England and Wales. According to the Knight Frank farmland index, overall values fell by 2.6% in the final quarter of 2016 and were down 9% year on year. The average price is now just under £7,500 per acre – although, over five years, prices are up by 23%; over 10 years, up by 127%; and over 50 years, up by 4,501%.

If you have a farm in Suffolk and it's the same size now as it was in 1920, you may be happy because it's worth so much more. You may also be miserable because you didn't buy the farms next door when they came up for sale.

All this information is called 'data'. Data is considered 'the new oil', a notion almost as mysterious as Bitcoin. Data won't heat your home, cook your food, charge your laptop or make your crops grow. All it seems to have in common with oil is that it's crude and hard to obtain. It also fuels the internet. Order a book from Amazon and somewhere in a cloud is data on your interest in Robert Frost, weight loss and box blight. If you have a debit card, your first dog's name and the make of your first car is in your databank. Whoever has access to my John Lewis data knows my history of desire better than my husband.

How does all this data affect how we live? If we know that NHS waiting times are up, but we don't analyse why and lack the wit and will to tackle the problem, then the data is like sand. If we know that 11,500 Africans enter Europe from Libya each month, but we don't analyse how the network of traffickers operates and use that knowledge to solve the problem, what's the point? If HMRC has the UK financial data on Uber, Airbnb and Amazon, but can't get those companies to pay tax in the country where they make their money, then the 'oil' is low grade and worthless. It might get us to spend more online with those pop-up ads, but it won't fasten the seatbelts. It won't save lives.

Still, the data bug is addictive. Since the news that China would no longer accept the UK's plastic waste, I've been digging around for the figures. We ship 500,000 tons of our plastic debris to China each year (2.7 million tons since 2012). However, a more important set of statistics has eluded me: how much plastic do we *import* from China each year? As a shopkeeper, I can tell you it's a lot. Nearly every plastic toy that comes into the UK is Made in China.

Paddington Bear may look Peruvian and speak English, but the adorable bear is made in China. Ditto those cute Peter Rabbit dishes, that Apple mouse, the iPhone and its cover, the Samsung landline phone, the packaging that keeps your exquisite *macarons* intact, the flowerpot that contains your Grown in England orchid and the 'bags for life'. It doesn't take a mathematical genius to see that we bring a heck of a lot more plastic into the UK from China than we ship back.

In data-speak, the word 'algorithm' means looking at the problem, putting data in a computer and getting the solution. I've got a simpler method. First, we praise China for its decision. Then, inspired by its commendable approach, we cease importing into the UK all plastic goods made in China. I think it's called a linear equation. Or just common sense.

February 7, 2018

THE BATTLE HYMN OF HOPE

A DREAM mid-winter break in London: the Charles I show at the Royal Academy (stupendous – don't miss it) and Elgar's Cello Concerto with Andreas Brantelid at the Royal Festival Hall (alas, you've missed it). Then the train back to Suffolk. Because I'm not a commuter I feel a frisson of excitement, the relief that something still works.

At Cambridge, a quartet of teenagers gets on. As they search their pockets for tickets, one boy confesses that on the journey to Cambridge he made an origami horse out of his ticket, forgetting he would need it at the exit. The chorus of 'Duh!' makes me smile. Then the conversation moves in a darker direction.

'Did you see the students in Florida on YouTube walking out of the school with their hands on their shoulders?'

'And Trump's saying "arm the teachers".'

'Can you imagine Mr P in History with a gun? He would have shot half the class by now.'

'Yeah. We'd have to hold class at Addenbrooke's.'

'Schools in America all have these drills called "Lockdowns". Code yellow means turn your mobile off and go to a classroom. Code red means lock the door and turn off the lights. Hide. Like a fire drill, but a *Kill Drill*.'

'What's weird is that you can get arrested if you buy a beer before you're 21, but when you're 18 you can buy a gun that can kill 17 people in six minutes!'

'The whole world is more violent now. Dunblane was here.'

'But Dunblane changed the law. It made handguns illegal. Americans think that the Second Amendment is one of the Ten Commandments.'

'Americans are in love with guns. They're gun crazy.'

'But do they love their guns more than their children? That's what the students in Florida are asking.'

I pretend to read while I eavesdrop, moved by their candour and knowledge. At Newmarket, they scramble off. I watch them: attractive, thoughtful, clever, funny, young. Friends. I'm still basking in their easy wit and warmth when I suddenly realise: they're the same ages as the students killed in Florida. This is news they identify with. Syria or #MeToo may feel remote, but dead 17 year olds are not. And I have to admit that, despite 24 hours in London, I have been watching the news of the shooting obsessively.

When the moral history of America is written, it will require a long chapter to uncover the story of the National Rifle Association (NRA), described by the writer Hal Crowther as 'a coalition of manufacturers and maniacs: one supplies the funding, the other supplies the fear'. It will need a writer like Mr Crowther, who has the narrowed pupil of a sharpshooter, to unravel the incestuous marriage of the American Congress and the NRA, the elected representatives who have sold their integrity down the river in exchange for NRA funding.

My pessimism about America's ballistic insanity is deep. I hardly dare write this but, in the days following the shootings, I began to feel a sliver of lightness in the dark. The impassioned words of the 'student survivors' have a resonance that has reverberated across the world.

Born into the world of social media, they are comfortable in front of the screen. They have technical deftness. It's thanks to them that we know that NRA membership provides discounts with companies like Hertz, Delta and United Airlines and a global hotel network. In the past two weeks, many of these companies have now dropped their associations. Now even gunshops and Walmart are showing the conscience and sanity that legislators have lacked.

It helps that the #NeverAgain movement has pushed websites into posting how much every elected representative in the US has received in financial contributions from the NRA – their share of the

$31 million the NRA spent on the 2016 presidential campaign. These are the first steps towards understanding why American lawmakers refuse to support even the sanest levels of gun control: raising the age to 21, registering guns and making 'bump stocks' and semi-automatic assault rifles illegal.

The American NRA, inspired by the British NRA, was formed in 1871 by generals from the Union army who were appalled that many of their young troops didn't know how to use a gun. The generals decided to bypass the National Guard because they believed going private was more efficient. Efficiency that, nearly 150 years later, allows a teenager to buy an AR-15, the semi-automatic assault rifle that left 17 dead and more than a dozen injured on Valentine's Day, and the weapon of choice in the last five major massacres in the USA.

Do I dare hope? In the 1960s, young students integrated all-white schools. They were the Freedom Riders integrating bus stations in the South. They registered black voters, and marched against the Vietnam War. They were angry, and their placards quoted St Augustine: 'Good anger is the daughter of Hope'. There was plenty to be angry about. They changed America.

I might be wrong. After the next massacre the same old prayers and condolences may be wheeled out. The #NeverAgain crusade won't rid the land overnight of the gun-worshipping Neanderthals who have spent years and millions rolling back civilisation, but the student survivors are being heard. They just might make it harder for a sad kid to acquire a weapon of war that fires 90 rounds a minute. That's a cause worth believing in.

March 7, 2018

My hope was misplaced.

America can't stop killing its children – and its teachers, relatives, members of congregations in churches, synagogues and mosques, because the Supreme Court interprets the Second Amendment as America's most sacred right. In the five years since the massacre at Marjory Stoneman Douglas High School in Parkland, Florida, which claimed the lives of 14 students and three staff members, another 110 people have been killed – including three children and three adults in an elementary school in Nashville.

CROSSING THE BRIDGE

READING Nora Ephron is like walking down a city street arm in arm, like two friends who never see enough of one another. On a grey day in the country when Spring seems to come and go and every page of the newspaper brings me down, I reach for her last collection of essays. The title provides instant comfort: *I Remember Nothing*.

The list of things Ephron doesn't remember is enviable. For example: she met Eleanor Roosevelt at Hyde Park, a prelude to a political internship at the Kennedy White House. She remembers nothing that the former First Lady said or what she wore. What she remembers: she got lost on the way. Every time she's been on the Taconic State Parkway since that day she has remembered getting lost on the way to meet Eleanor Roosevelt.

Ephron also marched on Washington to protest the war in Vietnam in 1967. The march on Washington was the most significant event of the anti-war movement. She went with a lawyer she was dating, and they

100

spent most of the day in their hotel room. She can't remember if they ever got to the Pentagon. I was also on that march with a boyfriend and his mother (no hotel room) and for years I've claimed that I 'stormed the Pentagon'. In fact, I was in the group of 40,000 behind the 30,000 that headed to the Pentagon. What I remember are the photographs of that march.

I'm pretty sure I heard Peter, Paul and Mary, but I don't remember what they sang. I never saw the dreamy protesters who stuck flowers in the barrels of the loaded guns of the MPs guarding the Pentagon, only the pictures that are now considered the icons of 'Flower Power'. That was in the days when MPs were Military Police. It would be another decade and another country before I learned that MP stood for something else.

I'm now crossing the bridge that connects remembering and forgetting, and I can report that it sways in the wind. Unlike the late and brainy Nora, who maintained she had never been able to remember, I have always prided myself on my memory. True, I've been lost on every car journey more than 10 miles from home, and I forfeited several interesting careers because I got lost on the way to the interview, but lodged in a corner of my brain has been the archives of friends' lives, political movements, 20th-century poets, themes from the movies and volumes I and II of Julia Child. Until quite recently I could tell you the name of all my primary-school teachers and where I sat in the class. I could draw up an inventory of the contents of every room in the houses of both my grandmothers, and recite all the state capitals and the Presidents. No longer.

There was a time when 'for better or for worse' was a solemn phrase in the marriage vows. My husband and I now vow to stick together because between us we have 'collective memory'. One of us will remember the name of the play by Tom Stoppard we didn't like (*The Hard Problem*); who the murderer is in *Foyle's War*; the writer we met in Crete 25 years ago (Antony Beevor); the restaurant on an island in Cork; and where Cosmo landed on D-Day.

Luckily, we don't duplicate each other's memory bank. His mental deposit box contains horticulture, military history, cricket and the grey partridge. Mine is stuffed with all things medical, culinary and American. He does flora, and I do fauna. We are both in the category of digital immigrants, latecomers to the digital age. We are neither LinkedIn or Snapchatters but we are fluent emailers (who isn't?) and we employ a legion of digital natives who keep us functioning in the 21st century. Again we have our specialities: he is master of the Sky Sports remote control, and I am as adept as any digital native at thawing the brain freeze with Google. As facts slide into the river that begins with L as far as you can recall, Google is the life raft of the forgetful.

Inspired by Nora, I made my own list of people I met and remember almost nothing about: Eudora

Welty, Lyndon Johnson, Dr Spock, Alger Hiss, Doris Lessing, Elie Wiesel, Margaret Thatcher and The Prince of Wales. What I remember are the anecdotes around these encounters that I have repeated for years. Not memory so much as history. I don't remember what they wore or what they said. I only wish I had paid more attention and written about it afterwards.

Just lately, I've come to perceive unforeseen benefits in the 'senior moment'. I think science will eventually discover that there is a part of the mind that filters out detritus the way the kidney filters out waste. When it ceases to function at full strength we let go of small resentments, remove the layers of regret and remorse. Example: I have had many hands wander on to my knee, quite a few squeezes of my backside, encounters with fairly literate fellows who thought 'no' meant 'maybe'. I vaguely remember the places, but I can't remember the names. Even if I could, my inner hashtag would be #MeToo/SoWhat?

I'm grateful for that fog which enables memories to lose their power. Memories can be as complicated as the Taconic State Parkway, and if you dwell too hard on them you will miss the exit that leads to the greater pleasure of the present.

April 4, 2018

LETTER TO MEGHAN

Dear Meghan,

Welcome to the AA Sisterhood – also known as the Anglo-American Sisterhood. Unlike the sisterhoods of your past – the best friends in your Catholic all-girls school, the sisters in your sorority at Northwestern University, your co-stars in *Suits* – this is a loose-knit sisterhood of free-born American women who are married to Englishmen.

Ours is a long tradition that began with the daughters of fortune, fabulously wealthy heiresses whose mothers guided their education and acquisition of languages and culture with the fastidious determination of orchid breeders. The prize was an English aristocrat, preferably a duke. Their mothers' success was recognised by Edward VII, who observed: 'American girls are livelier, better educated and less hampered by etiquette.'

Their intelligence and independent spirit was never their main appeal. The deal was this: rich American girls got titles, and titled young aristocrats got dollars.

We like to think that love came into it. I'm pretty sure that Cora Crawley (née Levinson), the Countess of Grantham in *Downton Abbey*, loved her husband, but it was three years after the large dowry tied to the marriage contract had saved his estate that the Earl realised he loved his American wife.

I am the beneficiary of a more enlightened age. Although my husband might have some regrets ('Your family has been in America 200 years and they don't even have a chain of gas stations?'), he was tender-hearted about my dowry, which consisted of a labrador called Adam and an apocalyptic vision of the future of British farming. In my twenties, I set out to save the world. By the time I married, in my thirties, I was ready to narrow my lens and turn an ancient Suffolk estate into a hotbed of utopianism.

I am a late-20th-century bride. The 21st-century American wife is more likely to have an MBA from Harvard than a dowry. The marriage contract has been replaced by the pre-nup, both as hard on the fragile structure of married love as you can get.

Some things are the same. I met my future husband at a dinner party in Battersea, a meeting carefully plotted by friends. You met Harry on a blind date at Soho House, discreetly arranged by friends. Although a generation apart, we share the good luck of marrying Englishmen when the age of incomprehensible manners and mores of class is confined to costume dramas.

Well, almost. You will already have discovered that

the crazy cousin locked in the attic in this country is 'class'. Americans who marry Englishmen are spared much because it is difficult to 'place' us, but, if America has never been as classless as it pretends, Britain has never been as rigid as its reputation.

Elizabeth Bennet was not of the same class as Mr Darcy – she cringes when her sisters and mother make that all too obvious – and in the fifth series of *Downton* it was revealed that Cora was the daughter of a Jewish dry-goods millionaire from Ohio, but the venom still lurks.

A couple of weeks ago, I emailed *The Times* because every photograph of you announced the price of your shoes/coat/bag. My rant about anti-Royalist, class-ridden claptrap didn't make the letters page, but the price tags have disappeared. Unfortunately, unless you take to wearing flour sacks, the politics of envy and price tags will be back. I hope you can ignore them.

Although you were born and raised in California and I was born in the Mississippi Delta, we both grew up in the shadow of Englishness. It begins with *Peter Rabbit* and *The Wind in the Willows* and leads to *Pride and Prejudice*. By the time I was 13 I had memorised *The White Cliffs of Dover*. I watched every episode on 'Masterpiece Theatre' and *Upstairs, Downstairs*; you've seen *Downton Abbey* and *The Crown*. As much as literature and Netflix may intrigue and inspire us, what really makes us who we are is rooted in our native soil.

You are a force of nature: a self-made, bi-racial woman, a graduate of a prestigious university, a successful actor whose passion for social justice has taken you all over the world. Your friends describe you as purposeful, loyal, life-loving and serious. You live in a global universe, but you're the best of what is American.

I used to think that the good American wife became, well, rather English. She softened her voice and practised a subtle osmosis to enable her to blend in. I've never learned the rules of cricket, but I willingly practise an intelligent silence during a Test match. I don't cry during Harrow songs – I cry during *Amazing Grace*, America's best-loved hymn, written by an Englishman – and get tearful at *God Save the Queen*. But, more and more, I've accepted George Orwell's belief that 'it is only when you meet someone of a different culture from yourself that you begin to realise what your own beliefs really are'. That's as true for Harry as it is for you.

I hope you will both stick to those beliefs because they come from the experiences that have made you who you are. They are the beliefs that you bring to each other, and they are greater than any dowry.

I'll be watching the wedding here in Suffolk. I will cry when Sheku Kanneh-Mason plays the cello and when I hear the ancient vows.

This comes with admiration from your new sisterhood and every wish for a long life of married love and fun,

Carla

May 2, 2018

THIS IMMORTAL NATION

THERE'S a line in *Sleepless Nights* by Elizabeth
Hardwick that comes as close to a personal motto as
I get: 'Make a decision and what you want from the
lost things will present itself.' Her decision was to
look back on her life and put together a scrapbook
of memories, dreams, portraits, letters and wishes.
Because she blended fact with invention, she called
her memoir a novel.

Owing to a lazy streak, I've never written a memoir,
but, like Miss Hardwick, I'm inclined to fuse fact with
fiction. Although I lack the sit-and-stay temperament
of a real writer, I have shuffled through memories and
past dreams, made a decision and got what I wanted.

It's in the old dairy section of a 400-year-old
Suffolk barn where a herd of pedigree Friesians was
once milked twice a day. The cows went before I came,
but, as I was raised with cows, I should thank Fortuna
for that. They can be demanding and anxious, living to
produce milk and more cows. I miss the sweet-smelling
idea of them, but not the dicey reality. In the milking-

parlour, I have fulfilled my dream: I have a bookstore.

Maybe 'bookstore' is too inventive. The Book Room is a dream that began in a pastoral childhood where life revolved around the Book-of-the-Month club, Reader's Digest condensed books and an annual trip to the Southern Baptist Bookstore 80 miles away. I was 17 before I entered a real bookstore, Brentano's in Washington DC. When I saw shelves with the writers from my own postage-stamp world – Faulkner, Welty, O'Connor, McCullers – next to Austen and Dickens, I felt the giddy glow of arrival.

Other bookshops have sparked a feverish *coup de foudre* – Shakespeare and Company on the Left Bank and Librairie Galignani on the rue de Rivoli – but the first bookshop I felt I could commit to for life was John Sandoe's in Blacklands Terrace, off the King's Road. I was living a few blocks away, an American with the dubious identity of a French *carte de travail* and a Mississippi driving licence. When John offered me an 'account' at Sandoe's, I felt as if I had been given citizenship.

I'm not the first American to fall in love with an English bookshop. Think of Helene Hanff's acerbic 20-year correspondence with a bookseller at 84, Charing Cross Road. My friend Rose in Virginia faithfully pays hefty postage to get books sent from Heywood Hill 'because they know what I like'. Visitors from Denmark and France spend whole days at Daunts.

The truth is, readers the world over are steeped in English literature. The English believe in an immortal nation, called Great Britain, bound together by place and by language. No one put this better than Shakespeare. Even in the doleful days of Brexit, we can turn to *Hamlet*: 'To be in or not to be in – now that's a very good question.'

When I opened my Book Room four years ago, bookshops were closing faster than village pubs. I was advised against it, but the bedrock of our farm diversification – a vineyard, restaurant, country store, farmers' market, garden – is my belief that people will always want to get out of the house and feel part of a community. I wanted to create a place folks came to for the smell of the hay and to find decent coffee, honest food, like-minded people and, well, good books.

From the beginning, I knew we had to outwit Amazon, so we put up hand-painted notices: 'If everybody buys all their books on Amazon, there won't be any literary, quirky bookshops.' We specialise in small English presses and stock almost all of the Everyman's Library, Eland (travel), Little Toller (Nature and countryside), Persephone (long-forgotten women writers), Notting Hill (essays) and Slightly Foxed, beautiful books you want to keep long after you've read them. Charlotte, literary and quirky herself, helps with the choosing, does all the ordering and keeps the records, in pencil, in spiral notebooks.

You may wonder what this has to do with Brexit or Miss Hardwick, who believed that it's much harder to write about what you like than what you *don't* like.

That's how I feel about Brexit. We can buck and snort until the cows come home about the ransom the EU aims to extract from Britain, how Brussels means to punish the UK as a warning to other members, how the Irish border has turned into a Trumpian wall, but all this whining distracts us from what we really want: a well-run country. We want our trains to run on time, a ticket to guarantee a seat and not cost the earth.

We want an education system that brings out the best in most of its children, and an NHS that values the doctors and nurses who take good care of us. We want a regime that taxes online shopping and cuts the rates that are turning our high streets into ghost towns; a country that is proud of its tolerance, diversity, resilience and gaiety, fills in potholes and no longer blames its problems on the meddling of the EU.

I reckon most people want post-Brexit Britain to be like a good bookshop: where poetry and science, history and Nature sit side by side; the chairs are comfortable; Keith Jarrett's piano plays in the distance; a sleeping dog blocks the doorway; and good coffee is next door.

Is it possible? Well, against the odds, this is a farm where books are growing faster than wheat and barley. It makes me feel humble and more convinced than ever that if you make a decision – and get on with it – you can have the country you want.

June 13, 2018

THE ARC OF HISTORY

ONE hot summer's day in early July, we opened the doors to our vineyard restaurant. The vineyard was three years old – the time it takes for vines to produce the grapes that make the wine – and the restaurant was 400 years old. That is to say, it was in a barn that was born in oak some four centuries earlier. We added a hard-wood floor and a new roof, put in thoughtful windows, installed a nearly new stainless-steel kitchen and opened for business.

Talk in this neck of Suffolk was that the American woman was nuts. Bets were taken on how long it would last. The bank manager spoke for many when he said: 'But you are nothing, *nothing in the middle of nowhere.*' Neighbouring farmers gazed into the distance and said they felt sorry for my husband.

That was 25 years ago; we now have 50 people on the payroll and, most days, that husband eats lunch in the cafe, a recipe for marital longevity if ever there was.

From the beginning, the menu had a subtle American accent. On the fourth Thursday in November, we celebrate Thanksgiving Southern style, with cornbread dressing, sweet-potato casserole and Norfolk black turkeys pan-smoked over grapevine prunings. Big letters on the menu advise the thankful to 'Save room for pie': pumpkin pie, pecan pie and apple pie with cinnamon ice cream.

Then there's the Fourth of July. I hang my old American-flag quilt over the balcony that once housed the seed dresser, but, otherwise, I'm sensitive to the fact that this day celebrates American independence from British rule. We serve Gloucester Old Spot hot dogs, Scottish lobster rolls, potato salad, ice-cold watermelon and strawberry shortcake. The menu sings 'freedom' more than 'independence', starting with *Charlotte's Web*: 'An hour of freedom is worth a barrel of slops' (said the goose to Wilbur the pig).

Then, in 2003, I left the flag quilt in the attic. No hot dogs, no roman candles like bombs bursting in air. No quotes from E. B. White or Thomas Paine, born 10 miles from this farm, whose revolutionary pamphlet *Common Sense* sparked the Declaration of Independence.

My enthusiasm for patriotic hoo-haw hit a lull because I believed the invasion of Iraq was a mistake, that Britain (Tony Blair) had provided gravitas and legitimacy to President Bush, and that the so-called coalition was a tragedy in the making. Soon after the fireworks of Shock and Awe, it was obvious that we could no more win the war in Iraq (ditto Afghanistan) than we could win an earthquake, but even then few could foresee the earthquake that would follow that war: Isis, Syria, Libya, Yemen...

113

This year, the flags are out again, although the news from America is crazier, more heartbreaking and more infuriating than I can ever remember. For the return of the flags, I can thank James Comey, the FBI director whom Donald Trump sacked after not getting the response he expected when he asked for his loyalty.

I went to hear the former director 'in conversation' with Emily Maitlis at the Barbican last week. Mr Comey, all 6ft 8in of him, divides opinion. The Hillary people blame him for their candidate losing; the Trump people blame him for turning the President down, getting himself fired and single-handedly triggering the Mueller investigation. How a man can have so many people mad at him and remain good-natured, articulate, graceful and believable is beyond me.

Mr Comey sees the history of America as an arc that moves ever upward, with plenty of troughs and ravines along the way. He has the clarity of a lawyer, but the confidence of a historian who has watched America go through dark times before. He reminded his audience of the McCarthy period, when the country was divided between those who accepted the device of loyalty oaths, witch hunts and the right to call anybody you didn't like a Communist and those who trembled at the thought. He asked us to remember the bomb in Birmingham, Alabama, that killed four young girls attending Sunday School.

Just when it looks as if humanity and civilisation are gone for good, he maintains that something happens:

114

the ground shifts, the people stand up and the graph of history moves. Did that happen last month when Americans learned that more than 2,000 children were taken from their mothers at the Mexican border? When the President cancelled 'due process' to asylum seekers? There is no guarantee. As long as people from south of the border seek to flee poverty and the violence of sectarian/drug/gang wars, there will be haunting scenes of desperate people. The struggle for survival is as old as humanity, and it's never been an easy journey.

I never thought I would hear an FBI director (albeit former) quote Martin Luther King, but it's Mr Comey's theme: 'The arc of history is long, but it bends toward justice.' It doesn't bend on its own, of course. It takes human action and reaction, exactly as it did nearly 250 years ago in a fallout over tea in Boston harbour.

It may seem as corny as Kansas in August, but, today, I'm hanging two ancient flags, one with only 48 stars, the other an old woollen Union Flag patched through the years by unknown hands. I'm celebrating the common language and values that unite these two countries, boosted by Mr Comey's belief that nothing terrible lasts forever.

The prize is a cloudless day, blueberry pie, babies napping on quilts in the shade. To paraphrase that goose: an hour of hope is worth heaps more than a barrel of slops.

July 4, 2018

HOME ON THE DUST BOWL

AFTER I left home, my father wrote to me once a week. He typed his letters, and I read them with the speed and carelessness of youth. Often, I'd find a letter in a coat pocket that had languished unopened for weeks. I saved all too few, but snatches reside in my head. In one, he wrote that he was reading *The Man without Qualities* by the Austrian novelist Robert Musil. I can smell from memory the magic marker he used to draw a thick black square around a quote from the protagonist Ulrich: 'One can't be angry with one's own time without damage to oneself.'

This was my father's way of warning me that if I spent all my time at demonstrations and writing incendiary articles for the college newspaper I would not graduate, I would be unemployable and I would die poor and lonely.

Ulrich's words have floated back to me because it's hard not to be angry about one's time during the long, hot summer of Brexit, Trump and Drought. I even see the signs of the damage: since the Referendum and the

116

election of Trump, I've gone from a size 12 to a size 14, my hair has lost its shine, and my eyebrows have faded from view. Even the rooms in this ancient house are looking down at heel.

Part of the problem is that my day begins with *Farming Today*, which is a cataclysmic account of climate change, dire predictions of the effect of Brexit on farming, interviews with farmers who keep 2,000 cows indoors and milk them three times a day, pigs dying of heatstroke, and sheep wasting away because grass has turned to straw. Long gone are Balzacian reports of the price of daffodils in Cornwall: farming today is Hell on Earth.

I perk up a little when *Today* comes on, not because the news is good, but because Martha Kearney's voice is balm against the chaos. She keeps me company in the kitchen, where I grind my bird-friendly, shade-grown beans. In fact, the best news to emerge during these fearful times is that seven cups of coffee a day are not detrimental to your health, although it might be hard on your loved ones.

My first cup gets me through *The Times* print edition and *The New York Times* online. The second is reserved for my Matins: a ceremonial read of the obituaries. I register the age of the distinguished departed – 94 seems to be the most popular – before I gaze at the name and then indulge in a patch of reverential peace as I wander through other lives (industrious, fertile and brave) and other times (arguably more turbulent than the summer of 2018).

Although I think of myself as an acolyte of the theologian Reinhold Niebuhr, best known for his *Serenity Prayer*, I've gone off the idea of asking God to grant me the serenity to accept the things I cannot change. The morning walk with the dog leaves us both panting, stopping to watch dust hovering over fields in which crops fight for survival. The reservoir looks more like a crater than a source of life, and in the glare of the sun I walk with my eyes shut.

Instead of serenely accepting that the farm looks as if it's appearing in a documentary on the Dust Bowl, I want to hog-tie and handcuff the foxy climate-change deniers and put them on a bonfire of their vanities, preferably in the empyrean fields of Suffolk, where temperatures reach 33ºC.

Then, there's Brexit. I voted Remain, but now I'm mad at everybody. I'm mad at the feebleness of the Remain campaign, and I'm mad at Leavers for their colossal ineptitude at planning the exit.

Whenever someone pontificates 'this is a Democracy and the people have spoken', I hear H. L. Mencken's version: 'Democracy is the theory that the common people know what they want and deserve to get it good and hard.'

The most obvious sign that my anger has damaged me is that I'm suffering from politically induced schizophrenia. One minute, I long to turn the clock back and wake up to find everything as it was before the Referendum; the next, I'm chomping for a no-deal exit. Brexit seems like war: easy to begin, but difficult to get out of.

And, forgive me for bringing it up, but there's Trump. Every evening at 6pm, we sit down with a glass of wine to watch the news. Then, at 7pm, Monday through Thursday, we watch *Beyond 100 Days*. This calls for another glass. It's the second glass that triggers an ominous realisation: I have become my parents.

During the Watergate era, their evenings began with the clack of the ice tray, then the crackle of bourbon cascading over ice. They had lived through the 1930s and the Second World War, but were mesmerised by what was going on in the White House. They believed in their inner souls that the future of the country was at stake, but that was nearly half a century ago and America is still standing, promising proof that countries generally outlive the men occupying the top spot.

Luckily, I'm married to an optimist, who expects it to rain any day now. He voted Remain, but is Born Again and predicts a bumpy year or two before the country flaps its wings and soars. He's convinced America will recover from the Trump years, and quotes Winston Churchill: 'You can always count on Americans to do the right thing – after they've tried everything else.'

I'll drink to that. Meanwhile, praise the Lord for screw tops.

August 1, 2018

119

DANGER INVITES RESCUE

WE'RE sitting around a table on a warm summer evening, lulled by that rarest of pleasures: eating outdoors by candlelight. The paisley tablecloth covers the gaps in the table's planks. A wine glass falls over. It knocks the candle, which lands on a napkin that catches fire. The lawyer among us nimbly smothers the fire. 'Danger invites rescue,' he says, as the flames disappear.

Ah, the irresistible music of metaphor. The rhythm of two nouns with two syllables connected by a genteel verb. To my ear, this is law as poetry.

Not that we know what it means. When the candle is re-lit and the glass re-filled, the lawyer tells us it was the judgment of Judge Cardozo in a 1921 New York case. He quotes from memory: 'The cry of distress is the summons to relief.'

He then gives the example of *Wagner vs. International Railway*. Riders are allowed to walk between cars while the train is moving. A rider falls through the cars. The plaintiff tries to help the fallen rider, and he himself is injured. 'The risk of rescue is born of the occasion. The emergency begets the man.' The judge doesn't say that it's a *moral* duty to attempt rescue, but the metaphor strongly suggests one ought to try.

This week, those words echoed in my mind. Not because I witnessed danger or attempted rescue, but because I saw the film of Ian McEwan's novel *The Children Act*.

To unwind further: the film is based on the book, and the book is based on the judgments of a real-life judge, who is a friend of the novelist and a friend of mine. The novelist's debt is no secret – in his acknowledgements, he writes: 'This novel would not exist without Sir Alan Ward, lately of the Court of Appeal, a judge of great wisdom, wit and humanity. My story has its origins in a case he presided over in the High Court in 1990, and another in the Court of Appeal in 2000.'

Mr McEwan is not unique among writers who have plundered the courtroom for literary fiction – think Charles Dickens, Harper Lee, John Grisham – but his focus is on the Family Court, where judges enter into lives at their most vulnerable and most intimate: love and love lost, marriages ending, children fought over and children neglected, religious wars and moral battles – difficult ordinary life colliding with extraordinary events.

Out of this morass of human bewilderment, the

judge is required to look into the distance and to see up close, to be both pragmatist and prophet. Add to the mix 'secular poet' and you get Sir Alan, the High Court judge who ruled that an emergency blood transfusion should be given to a 15-year-old boy suffering from leukaemia, despite his parents and the boy refusing treatment because they were practising Jehovah's Witnesses.

In *The Children Act*, the judge decides to go and see the boy. (With poetic licence, Mr McEwan makes his judge a woman, played by Emma Thompson in the film.) This Sir Alan did in real life, suspending proceedings and taking a taxi through London on a September evening to the Hammersmith Hospital. Unlike Mr McEwan's version, they didn't discuss poetry and the boy didn't play a violin. The real boy's passion was not for Yeats, it was for Tottenham Hotspur. There was no singing, but a lively discussion of football.

After an hour together, Sir Alan returned to the court and overruled the objections of the boy and the parents. The boy was transfused and he survived. Months later, Sir Alan took the boy and his father to a Tottenham game, where they sat in the directors' box and the boy met his football heroes.

You could say that the boy was saved by the law, by the Children Act of 1989: 'When a court determines any question with respect to... the upbringing of a child... the child's welfare shall be the court's

122

paramount consideration.' But we depend on the judges to understand and foresee the child's welfare. We are only a civilised and kind country if those who make these decisions are humane and wise.

Both the novel and the film open with an earlier case of Justice Ward, the case of conjoined twins. If they are not separated, both will die. However, if they are separated, the weaker one will perish, for the child has virtually no brain, a weak heart and, in the words of the judge, 'no lungs to cry with'.

This case was also brought to court because of religious objections. Justice Ward's introductory remarks are now famous: 'This court is a court of law, not of morals, and our task has been to find, and our duty is then to apply, the relevant principles of law to the situation before us.' Like Judge Cardoza, Justice Ward doesn't say that it is the moral duty to rescue, but his actions and his judgments imply humanely that one *ought* to try. It is not a court of morals, but the courtroom, like life, is filled with moral complexity.

In a land where we live and die by the Rule of Law, it's useful to be reminded – even if by a novel or a film – that the 'law' is a human institution. The law can be an ass, but it is the best structure for civilisation that humans have come up with. Sometimes, it is even delivered with the clarity and beauty of poetry.

Danger invites rescue, and we are all the better for it.

September 5, 2018

123

SOUVENIRS DU TEMPS PERDU

I'VE loved the long, hot summer, but autumn is my season. Mellow fruitfulness restores my faith: there's something simple and true about ripening apples glistening in the October sun, especially after the days in August when a miniature version of the crop gave up and fell to earth. Getting to the chicken house was like walking through landmines, each one loaded with wasps.

For days, we scooped them up and wheeled them over to the compost heap. I hoped word might get around and the rats that spend their evenings in the orchard munching corn would head over to the Compost Bar and get drunk on fermented apples. In the thick summer heat I forgot that the resident boy who spent summer evenings shooting rats grew up and left home 10 years ago.

I grew up with the proverb 'If you've got chickens, you've got rats'. I also know the 11th Commandment: elevate all feeders and waterers 22in off the floor. But God's creatures, great and small, are beneficiaries of evolution, and rats are clever, agile and determined – 22in means nothing to today's opportunists. Think of Templeton, the rat that lives under Wilbur's trough in *Charlotte's Web*: 'The rat had no morals, no conscience, no scruples, no consideration, no decency, no milk of rodent kindness, no compunction, no higher feeling, no friendliness, no anything.'

There is one thing worse than farmyard rats, however. City rats.

Ella Fitzgerald might love Paris in the springtime, but not me. I love Paris in late September when Parisians outnumber tourists, the air is crisp, and even the waiters are cheerful after their month in the country. I stay in the 15th with my friend Judith, and we visit old haunts from the days when we were girls of slender means and lived on the wrong side of Montparnasse.

Last week, we had the dramatic new Fondation Louis Vuitton and the majestic Musée Picasso almost to ourselves. We're old enough to remember when the Marais wasn't chic, and we traced our steps from Picasso to the Place des Vosges and the *bistro du vin* Ma Bourgogne. We drank silky Fleurie, and ate an *assiette de charcuterie* from the Auvergne. Bliss it is to find everything just as it was, but when it's even better 'tis surely heaven.

Mellowed by Beaujolais, we decided to walk home under a Paris moon, crisscrossing the Seine, stopping in the square in front of Notre-Dame. At first, I thought the movements were cats: cat families and kittens everywhere. 'This is like Rome used to be,' I said, before I realised that these were not wild felines. Not cats but... rats. Not a dozen rats, not even 100 rats, but 1,000 rats. A plague of rats. In the centre of Paris. In front of the Cathedral of Notre-Dame.

When President Macron was in Salzburg displaying manners not unlike Templeton as he addressed the Prime Minister of the United Kingdom, his own capital city was occupied by a marauding army of *Rattus norvegicus* (distinct from the *Rattus rattus*, blamed for the Black Death). And what an army: dressed in coats of lustrous grey-brown, these invaders were bold, aggressive and very fat.

My *nostalgie de la boue* hit a lull, and we headed to the taxi rank. Safe inside our rat-proof Renault, I asked: 'When did this happen?'

Judith began to explain that some blame it on the flooding of the Seine, but the rat invasion began before the floods. Another theory: their underground life became too crowded, so they began living above ground. Articles in *Le Figaro* blame the rise in people living on the streets; *Le Monde* blames the restaurants that leave their rubbish out each night.

Suddenly, our driver growled: '*Non! Non! Non! C'est l'Union Européenne!*'

Like a scene in a French movie – or a London cab – he growls louder: 'Brussels! They take away the good rat poison!' He tells how, in the old days, the park employees put lethal pellets into the burrows, and the metro and sewer workers sprinkled poison along the underground tunnels used by the rats. The poison was sticky, and when the rats licked themselves they absorbed the poison. *'Morts! Fichus!'*

We hang on to our seatbelts as he describes the EU *déclaration* that the poisons were a danger to cats, children and pregnant women. *'Comment? Dites-moi! Comment?'* Certainly not as dangerous as the rats that now infest Paris and the Seine. *'Toutes les trois semaines!'* he growls. Rats breed every three weeks; when the child rats are six weeks old they have sex and make babies. *'C'est une guerre et nous avons perdu!* The rats have taken over!'

But what about the black bait boxes that are everywhere? Outside the Louvre, around the Eiffel Tower (and, I might add, in our barns and grain stores). *'Bof! Ornamental!* Symbols of *les imbéciles* in Brussels!' Parisian rats have *'bon goût'*, and naturally prefer baguette with Camembert to pellets in a black box. When street cleaners investigated 500 bait boxes, they didn't find a single one that had been breached by a rat. *'Pas un!* Not one! *Rien!'*

He admires the British for leaving the EU ('Bravo! *Bon travail*!') because he thinks the French are finished. When the rat catchers (mainly north African) asked for stronger poison, 25,000 Parisians signed a petition protesting against the 'genocide of rats'.

'Rat rights! *Imbéciles*!'

At St Pancras, I keep an eye out for rats. I won't see one until I'm back in Suffolk. In my absence, the battle to ratify the divorce papers from the EU has stalled, but the utopian vision of a post-EU, rat-free Britain lives on. It seems what's needed is arsenic – and the sound defeat of the Rat's Rights party.

October 3, 2018

A FAREWELL TO ARMS

A FEW years ago, the wife of my husband's first cousin sent me a slender essay by her American grandfather. Written at Christmas 1921 in Sewanee, Tennessee, it tells of his arrival five years earlier at Oxford as a Rhodes Scholar: 'In October 1916, I entered Oxford – War Oxford – a golden setting devoid of jewels. It was as a stage set for a mighty drama whose actors failed to appear... a sleeping city of wonder, with towers and spires over which the spell of an evil genie had cast an unwonted stillness.'

Lawrence Faucett had grown up in Chattanooga, gained a bachelor's degree in Divinity from the University of the South in Sewanee, and in 1916 was ordained as an Episcopalian minister before being awarded a Rhodes scholarship. Oxford in the third autumn of war was a sad and desolate place, but the young American looked back on those days with 'a sense of pleasure mixed with wonder, a sense of happiness mingled with a strange sadness'. He felt 'grateful to England for one thing above others. From October 1916, until April 1917, no Englishman in whose home I was a guest ever broached America's attitude to the war as a subject for conversation.'

In 1916, most Americans wanted no part of the 'European war'. Even after the RMS *Lusitania*, sailing from New York to Ireland, was sunk in May 1915 by a German submarine with the loss of nearly 1,200 lives, including 128 Americans, President Woodrow Wilson called on the USA to remain neutral. He was re-elected the following year on the slogan 'He kept us out of war!'. But not for much longer. The Germans continued to expand their submarine warfare, and on April 2, 1917 the President asked Congress for a declaration of war with the solemn words: 'It is a war against all nations.' Four days later, Congress declared war on Germany.

For most Americans, the First World War is America's forgotten war. It barely exists in the fog of modern memory. Portraits of my great uncles John Adcock and Forrest Cooper in their uniforms hung over the mantelpieces of my childhood, but I never asked about the war they had fought in. It wasn't until I was at university, and focused on Vietnam, that I learned that, in 1917, more than two million American men were sent overseas to France to fight a war in which 116,708 American soldiers died and 200,000 were wounded.

Like many Americans, much of my knowledge of the war came from *A Farewell to Arms*, Ernest Hemingway's story of a wounded American soldier and his doomed love affair with an English nurse. The novel had added poignancy because we knew that Hemingway had experienced the war first-hand as a volunteer who served in Italy as an ambulance driver with the American Red Cross. In June 1918, two weeks before his 19th birthday, he was wounded by Austrian mortar fire. Like his character Lt Frederic Henry, Hemingway fell in love with a Red Cross nurse when he was recuperating in an Italian hospital.

The literature we knew that decried the war came from British poets – Rupert Brooke, Wilfred Owen, Siegfried Sassoon. Hemingway's *Farewell* was a uniquely American argument combining austere realism, disillusion and powerful language.

My generation took more from the novel than the message 'war is hell', however. Before Hemingway's young lieutenant returns to the front, the English nurse, Catherine, gives him a St Anthony medal, patron saint of miracles and lost causes. Fifty years later, St Anthony was the medal given by girlfriends to their young men shipping out to Vietnam.

The men who survived the First World War saw their lives – and those of their children and grandchildren – change course. When America entered the war in April 1917, Caroline McLaren's grandfather, Faucett, joined the British services rather than return home to enlist. In July 1918, he married an Englishwoman, and after Armistice Day they returned to Oxford, where he resumed his Rhodes scholarship.

When Faucett was writing about his memories of Oxford at war, he was a professor of English at the University of the South in Sewanee. He would go on to plant the English language throughout the world, particularly in China and Japan, and be recognised as one of the most innovative pioneers in the teaching of English as a foreign language. He died, aged 86, working on his final book, based on his own translations of the writings of Confucius.

This farming estate in Suffolk is a more modest legacy of the First World War. My husband's first cousin entered Oxford in 1911, and, with the rest of his generation, was swept into the horrors of war. In 1914, he joined the London Regiment and went with them to Gallipoli. He was wounded but, in May 1916, returned to the Near East, where he served without home leave until August 1919.

Like the poets who dreamt of deep meadows and hares about the corn, Frank Heilgers dreamt of fields of wheat and cows grazing peaceably. When he returned, he bought Wyken, a rambling farmhouse that needed rebuilding and 1,000 acres that struggled to show a profit. In 1931, he was elected to Parliament and continued as the Member for Bury St Edmunds until a foggy day in January 1944, when the train carrying him to London was ploughed into by another train. He was 51.

I am writing this in a place that was the dream of a soldier who fought in the war to end all wars. A long and brutal war called the Great War. A war that ended 100 years ago on a sepia November day and changed the course of history.

November 7, 2018

A FESTIVAL OF MEMORY

'IF I could work my will,' said Scrooge indignantly, 'every idiot who goes about with "Merry Christmas" on his lips should be boiled with his own pudding, and buried with a stake of holly through his heart.'

You don't have to be a paid-up Dickensian to know who spoke those blood-curdling words. The mean old miser is as much a part of our collective Christmas memory as holly, wreaths, mistletoe and carols. Every year, a new edition of *A Christmas Carol* appears, with illustrations that have become more lavish and kinder than in Christmas Past.

My original version consisted of black line drawings that were as scary as the words. I can remember Scrooge's terrified face when he sees Marley's ghost, the fog of London replaced by the haze of Chesterfields as my father smoked and read to us.

Christmas is a festival of memory. We may lose track of names, places and dates, but we remember the words to carols, the fixed menu of the feast that marks the day, the story that begins with the unpromising words: 'And it came to pass in those days, that there went out a decree from Caesar Augustus, that all the world should be taxed.'

It doesn't take much to trigger Christmas memories. Mine were set off this week by a book called *I Remember* by Joe Brainard. First published in 1970, *I Remember* is a cult classic that had passed me by. Fortunately, Notting Hill Editions, publishers dedicated to the best essays past and present, have given it new life. As I read Brainard's resonant memories, I felt like a witness to a meteor bursting across the winter sky.

The timeline of Brainard's observations covers the 1950s, 1960s and 1970s, and each memory begins with the refrain 'I remember'. Inevitably, his memories activate one's own, and you begin to roam around your lost worlds of time and place. Two things help: Brainard's belief that 'everything is interesting, sooner or later'; and Christmas itself, the siege of togetherness, when the memory's pinnacle of happiness sits side by side with the hopes and fears of all the years.

I remember going with my grandmother to the bootlegger each autumn to buy whisky for her Christmas fruitcakes. Mississippi was the last state to repeal Prohibition, and she was the widow of the county prosecuting attorney and a Southern Baptist. She justified her illegal purchase with her conviction that her Christmas fruitcakes were the birthday cake of Jesus.

I remember writing to Santa Claus and asking for

cowboy boots and a Davy Crockett hat with a real racoon tail.

I remember the ecstasy of Midnight Mass and the glow of incense and candlelight.

I remember the scrapbook I received one year. The only pictures I put in it were of horses and dogs and a photograph of Anthony Eden I tore out of *Life* magazine. I thought he was more handsome than Elvis. I was seven and had never been north of Tennessee.

I remember Christmas records: Perry Como, the Vienna Boys Choir, Barbra Streisand.

I remember my first Christmas in England. On the train journey into London, I was shocked to see shanty towns more pitiful than any in the Delta. I thought of what Christmas was like there as I took in the beauty and grandeur of A Festival of Nine Lessons and Carols at King's. Several years would pass before I learned that the 'slums' were allotments, and no one lived in the shacks.

I remember my first married Christmas in Suffolk. The house was filled with my English husband's family, and I did all the cooking: turkey with cornbread dressing and sweet-potato casserole. No bread sauce. No chipolatas. Instead of Christmas pudding, I made Jane Grigson's frozen lemon souffle. Despite their secret longings, my new in-laws practised a tactful silence.

I remember when Sam was little and we had a stand of wayward conifers in our woods. My husband went out early in the morning and decorated a small tree with weighted candleholders and candles. At noon, we headed off with a Thermos of hot chocolate. Just before we reached the tree, I'd distract Sam as his father ran ahead to light the candles. Hand in hand, we'd come upon a magical candlelit tree. This tradition continued until Sam was more interested in felling the tree with the axe than in the candles.

I remember when my father came for Christmas, the year after my mother died. He brought us wool sweaters from L. L. Bean that we still wear and a gallon of Jack Daniels to lace our eggnog. He brought Sam a Davy Crockett hat with a real racoon tail. Once upon a time, it had been mine.

I remember the verb 'to give' – Christmas was a time of giving. No one said they had 'been gifted' or spoke of 'gifting'. It was a much better time for language.

I remember when the Christmas season began in December, not September. Everybody liked that better.

I remember that my mother always decorated our Christmas tree when we were at school – it was only on television that happy families did it together. Now, I decorate the tree and spend hours setting out many crèches. I begin with *Once in Royal David's City* and coffee, and by the time I lay Baby Jesus in his manger Judy Garland is singing *Have Yourself a Merry Little Christmas* and it's eggnog and whisky. I feel happy and sad.

I remember being intimidated by the ruthless

Christmas gamesmanship of the family I married into. Now I, too, love the games. This year – with gratitude to Joe Brainard – I'm adding a new one: the Remember Game. The fire is lit, Joan Baez and Elvis are singing carols, fruitcake and mint tea are plentiful, and the oldest person goes first. The subject is Christmas, and the only rule is: every sentence must begin 'I remember'.

December 5, 2018

IV

What Ain't To Be Just Might Happen

IF NOT NOW, THEN WHEN?

IN the beginning, we didn't know it was the beginning. Our worries were elsewhere. After the wettest winter in memory, our fields of winter wheat looked like the bayous of Louisiana. The machinery barn stood tomb-like, the green hulks of machinery inside too heavy to go on the land without causing grievous harm to the soil beneath the water.

I am a woman who spots a rock in the middle of the road and says 'apocalypse'. When I married, my dowry consisted of a vision of farming on the edge of the abyss. I'd barely said 'I do' before I whispered: 'Trouble ahead. Diversify the farm.' I brought my son up on Grimm's fairy tales and *The Worst Case Scenario Survival Guide*. The larder looks like a well-stocked bomb shelter, because I've never walked out of Waitrose without a supply of loo paper, light bulbs and dog food.

And yet, and yet – I left it too late to stock up on paracetamol and hand sanitiser. What kept me awake at night wasn't the life and death part of the story, but fear for the livelihoods of the 50 people on our payroll.

I was drenched in anxiety about how they – and this farm that we had, indeed, diversified – would survive. The original advice – to 'avoid pubs and restaurants' – left farmers who'd converted their 16th-century barns into restaurants in darkness. There was no ray of light until the message 'Lockdown' and the Chancellor's 80% 'furlough' lifeline.

The lockdown was the real beginning of our coronavirus reality: the day a thriving community of chefs, waiters, shop staff, vineyard crew, gardeners, stall holders in our farmer's market – and customers – no longer showed up. Overnight, a farming community that goes back to Domesday turned into a ghost town.

The silence and the absence leads to a complete loss of a sense of time. I try to see it as a gift. I cook one-pot meals, and take from the cellar bottles once reserved for birthdays and anniversaries. Like a pop star on *Desert Island Discs*, I decide to read *War and Peace*, and I listen to old favourites: Janet Baker, Bryn Terfel, Johnny Cash, Joni Mitchell, Glenn Gould.

Some evenings, I wander over to the barn and sit in the empty space. English tithe barns are like secular cathedrals, and this one has withstood wars, pandemics, epidemics and decades when the farm lost money every single year. Now, empty of any purpose but survival, it feels as prayerful as a country church.

Each morning, I wake up to an inbox of emails from friends in America. I save them until I've fed the chickens and made coffee. Some are so funny I watch them over and over. Some are so shocking – a field hospital being erected in Central Park, numbers that are worse than the day before – that I freeze in disbelief. It takes an email from rural Georgia finally to get me to abandon my laptop.

One-time editor of a small-town newspaper in the Mississippi Delta, courageous columnist and long-time good friend Mac Gordon sends me his 'Corona Advice'. I'm not looking for advice, but reading it makes me think: 'If not now, then when?'

He begins: start making three stacks of documents. The first stack requires your will. Find it. Read it. Bring it up to date. Make sure all your heirs are still alive and your executors still willing and able to execute. If you haven't arranged a 'lasting power of attorney' or a living will, think of it as 'now or perhaps never'. Send off amendments and changes of heart to your solicitor and get the legal ball rolling. This stack is also the place for your List of Wishes. I've lost or given away half the stuff on my list, and some of the recipients have wandered off, but this is a job that always cheers me up.

Stack number two is the financial matter: insurance policies; direct debits; bank statements; credit cards; tax returns; subscriptions with broadband, Netflix, mobile phone. Make a list of all your passwords. Make lots of copies. The copy taped to my laptop yields more serenity than yoga.

For the third stack, you might want to buckle up. Start with locating your birth certificate, your marriage licence, a couple of photographs (young you, older you). If you think it is morbid and depressing to think about your human mortality, now is a good time to get over that, because this last stack is your obituary. The one you write. Nobody knows the story better than you do. Begin with your full name, your date and place of birth, your parents' names, where you grew up, education, marriages, careers, children, achievements, beliefs. Don't feel shy or uneasy about this. Think of it as a gift for those you leave behind. It's not a memoir, but a fact sheet that has no word limit. It brings a whole new meaning to the word 'deadline', but the time to do it is now.

Focusing, indeed accomplishing anything, in the shadow of this evil pandemic isn't easy. The handsome volume of *War and Peace* remains unopened, but the stacks of my documents have the heft and usefulness of a bushel basket. Now I'm even thinking of writing my epitaph, inspired by Jan Struther (the real Mrs Miniver), who wrote her own:

> One day my life will end; and lest
> Some whim should prompt you to review it,
> Let her who knows the subject best
> Tell you the shortest way to do it:
> Then say, 'Here lies one doubly blest.'
> Say, 'She was happy.'
> Say, 'She knew it.'

April 15, 2020

SHELTERING IN PLACE

BACK to the beginning, when it felt as if it was only me and Tom Stoppard. Writing in *The Spectator* in early March, he confessed that, if it weren't for the terror behind it, 'social isolation without social disapproval' is the life he has always dreamed of. This is the only #MeToo movement to which I belong. When I wake up and remember that I have nothing more urgent on the horizon than feeding animals, I feel a swoosh of contentment. It may sound tactless, but I've long believed that the most beautiful word in the English language is 'cancelled'.

If 'sheltering in place' sounds like poetry to me, it is not a poem my husband has read. Never a resistance fighter – his unwritten political memoir will be called *Moderate, with Fog Patches* – he insists that he will not be incarcerated during his twilight years. As soon as the lockdown shows signs of softening, he vows to defy the age ban and march forth to Brooks's, the Beefsteak, the London Library, the Woody Plant Committee.

'You're really storming the barricades,' I say. He

thinks I underestimate the implications of this state-sanctioned discrimination. 'The Queen can never again appear in public!' 'Charles denied his coronation in Westminster Abbey!' 'The House of Lords finished!'

The intimate lockdown reveals our dormant prejudices and different pulse rates. I see coronavirus as one of the most transformative events in modern history, a crisis that reveals our fragility as human beings. He sees it as a serious historical event, but not one that should fundamentally change the way of the world. It seems it takes a pandemic to sharpen the points of your compass. It also opens the memory bank.

Once a year in my elementary school, our teacher would put up a large poster in our classroom. Under the words HELP FIGHT POLIO, a wide-eyed little girl or boy looked up at us, leaning bravely on their crutches and wearing a metal brace on one leg. It was March of Dimes week, and the whole school filed into the hall to watch the film *The Polio Story*.

As soon as the lights went out, we heard the sound of sirens. We sat in the dark until the ambulances appeared on the screen, racing through city streets, bumping along dirt roads, crossing wooden bridges all across America. They were carrying children to hospitals.

Scary as the sirens were, what really terrified us were the small heads like our own sticking out of the iron lungs, long metal tubes that breathed for the children whose lungs had stopped working. Some children spent a year in the iron lungs. Some spent the rest of their lives in them. A man who looked like my grandfather told us he had got polio when he was 39 and that he started the March of Dimes to raise money for research and crutches and wheelchairs for crippled children. We didn't know he was President Roosevelt, because he died before we were born.

Back in the classroom, our teacher would ask us if we knew anyone who'd had polio. Most hands went up, and I always thrust mine high in the air. 'My big sister had polio when she was five!' I announced proudly. Her case was mild, and dancing lessons made her legs stronger.

March of Dimes week planted the virus deep in our hearts. We learned that it was invisible and highly contagious, how it was important to wash our hands with soap and hot water. We saw pictures of bus and train drivers wearing protective masks, and entire neighbourhoods with signs that read 'Polio! Quarantined!' Although we watched it every year, we always found it spooky. We loved the ending. Adorable monkeys, young mice, guinea pigs and rabbits in cages twitched and hopped as Dr Salk explained that animals such as these had made it possible for him to discover and test a vaccine that was safe for us. We were lucky children who would not get polio.

Neither coronavirus nor Covid-19 rolls off the tongue – my Southern cousins call it 'Rona' – but more people have died from it than polio, edging towards 30,000 in the UK at the time of writing and 250,000 worldwide. Memories are short. The first beneficiaries of the Salk and Sabin vaccines were the 70-plus folk, the generation that bypassed the fear, the bewilderment and the suffering of a virus called poliomyelitis or infantile paralysis – the generation that's now complaining loudest.

Some of us (me and Sir Tom) may have a greater capacity for solitude, but for the vigorous and gregarious (my husband and co) patience is required. The Queen will still reign over us and, when the day comes, Prince Charles will be crowned in Westminster Abbey. If its members continue calmly to shelter in place, the Garden Society will gather again in St James's. A vaccine looks hopeful, but this is no time for the Privileged Old to incubate feelings of discrimination and persecution. The most liberating thing we can do is to create a more accommodating wind vane to our compass.

PS: My sister who had polio lives in Maryland, where she is self-isolating with her husband. I had an email this morning: 'We're doing fine. Maryland hasn't peaked yet, but should soon. I'm blown away by the folks who don't believe this is real and say it's just a government takeover created by the liberal news media. Easy to stay quarantined when you think about people like that out there.'

May 13, 2020

LONG LIVE THE LAND
OF SHOPKEEPERS

A FEW years ago, we spent three days lugging three generations of books down from the attic. When I came here as a bride, these once-loved books were on the shelves, but the marital rite of merging libraries – making way for the arrival of William Faulkner, Eudora Welty, Flannery O'Connor, Carson McCullers – sent into exile the rows of books on shooting, fishing, cricket and cattle farming in Argentina.

The Attic Collection occupied every table in the house. A book dealer from Bungay was coming to have a look and, I hoped, take them away. My husband saw commercial potential; I hoped merely to avoid the tragedy of the books bringing down the ceiling in the rooms below.

I say 'a few years ago', but that's wrong. It was before Amazon and www.abebooks.com changed the landscape, back in the days when every town had a secondhand bookshop where you could spend hours lost in the quiet, claustral shelves. These bookshops were as English as the village church and the pub, and the best ones understood the antiquarian book dealers' iron rule: good books don't pull bad books up; bad books pull good books down. Bookshop shelves not regularly purged of junk will soon look like a junk shop. Ditto, I fear, bookshelves at home.

The book dealer arrived in a Volvo station wagon the size of a bus, loaded with empty banana boxes, the perfect shape and heft for shifting books spine-side-up. Despite the car's size, he had to make two trips to haul his purchases. The following day, he returned the banana box that contained the 12-volume set of *The Standard Cyclopedia of Modern Agriculture*, edited by Prof Sir Robert P. Wright. In the night, I'd suffered an acute attack of Sellers' Remorse. Note: these volumes take up 2ft of shelf space, and I've yet to get beyond Vol 1: *Abattoir to Auricula*.

The memory of this transaction makes me wistful. You're now more likely to find a farmer who ploughs with Suffolk Punches than a secondhand book dealer. Except for *vaut-le-voyage* Hay-on-Wye, secondhand bookshops have all but vanished, and the antiquarian book trade is in terrible shape.

Finding an out-of-print book online is satisfying, but it lacks the serendipity of coming across a book you weren't looking for. No bell rings as the door opens, no incense of old books fills the air, and there's no conversation with the owner who left a poorly paid job in publishing to fulfil his dream of running a bookshop. Now, the book-loving proprietor stores his/her stock in every room in the house and garage and spends his/her day sitting at a computer.

If I'm reading the runes, the country denounced by Napoleon as 'a land of shopkeepers' may soon cease to be a land of shopkeepers. Instead, we will be a land of online traders, with websites, warehouses and delivery vans. The reassuring banknotes with the profile of The Queen will be replaced by PayPal.

I confess I spent two years heading in that direction. With the warning 'the future of retail is online' ringing in my ears, I met weekly with my shop manager. We created a list of 'Wyken classics' that were unique to us and not made in China. We searched environmental packaging, met with photographers, studied the who and how and gazed at sites we liked – our favourite was Toast.

Then, one day, I got fed up: 'People need to go somewhere. I want the shop to be one of the places you want to be!' The staff are too young to remember the old V&A Museum advertisement – 'an ace caff with quite a nice museum attached' – but that's how I felt about the restaurant and the shop. And so we muddled along. The vines produced grapes, the chefs cooked, the people came and bought stuff. Life was good until lockdown. Overnight, our carefully curated world stopped.

It took my son, working 'from home' in their cottage in Firle, and my daughter-in-law, a doctor on the frontline in A&E, one weekend to create an online shop. In three days, we sold an entire pallet of our Good Dog Ale with a 'best by' date of May 30. In a week, we sold £10,000 of wine that was languishing in the bonded warehouse next to the old dairy. Now, they're adding more stuff to the site. I haven't lifted a finger. It didn't stop there. With no date for the restaurant to re-open, they hired a 1989 Citroën pizza van that arrived here on a flatbed truck. We now sell wood-fired sourdough pizza in the farmyard. At first, it was 'takeaway pizza until we re-open'. Now it's another arm to the farm diversification, specialising in pizza made with ingredients from the estate: smoked muntjac and wild garlic, confit pheasant and asparagus.

Will we go back to being a 'bricks-and-mortar' shop? Which, in our case, is a 400-year-old barn that outlived its usefulness as a shelter for cows and hay in the 1950s, then became redundant in the 1970s when farm machinery grew too big for its humane dimensions. Have shops you can wander around simply outlived their usefulness?

Strangled by rents and rates, many were on life-support long before the arrival of Covid-19, but now fear and anxiety are added to the picture. When Waterstones announces that any book touched by human hands will be removed and quarantined for 72 hours, it makes the most intrepid booklover hesitate. When you can't try on the shoes or stroke the Scottish sweater, will you simply order online as everyone under 30 now does? I can't get that Joni Mitchell song out of my head:

> So they paved paradise
> Put up a parking lot...
> Don't it always seem to go
> That you don't know what you got 'til it's gone...

June 10, 2020

A MORALITY TALE

Behold, I tell you a mystery.
We shall not all sleep, but we shall all be changed,
in a moment,
in the twinkling of an eye...
I Corinthians, chapter 15, verses 51-52

ALTHOUGH I grew up in a land where scripture was planted into our mouths with our first set of teeth, the language of King James is no longer on the tip of my tongue. I feel about the loss the way Julian Barnes described his lack of faith: 'I don't believe in God, but I miss Him.'

Still, on the bewildering journey of coronavirus, Corinthians has come back to me. Like all Biblical prediction, timing is more poetic than precise. Wise men and women – epidemiologists, economists, psychologists – predict we will all be changed, but, when it comes to 'the twinkling of an eye', they tend to be vague.

The ways Covid-19 will change us are as innumerable as they are inconceivable. Some changes are already in place. Working from home is no longer a privilege to be negotiated, but an institution. Avoiding the misery of commuting will cut pollution and lift happiness. It will boost the movement for faster broadband in the middle of nowhere, and cut the sales of cars and petrol. If you live in the countryside, you will be amazed. If you are a car dealer or own a chain of petrol stations, you won't be so happy, but you may have more free time.

Visits to the GP's surgery are also being transformed. There's even a word for it: 'telemedicine' means that you can book in for a video conference with your GP instead of sitting in a crowded waiting room where everyone looks worse off than you are, germs are all-pervasive and the background rattle of Radio 2 makes each visit feel more life-threatening than the symptoms that brought you there.

Old folks will no longer struggle to make the journey, but sit next to a dutiful son or daughter who can join in the call. Common ailments can be diagnosed online, and prescriptions filled, re-filled and delivered. This is a small revolution that will make us calmer and healthier.

Another change now causing panic, but with the potential to be a good thing, is in the world of higher education. Our universities are now so hooked on the easy money of foreign students, especially from China, that nothing short of a global pandemic could wean them off their addiction. At Manchester University, one in eight students is Chinese; at Liverpool, it's one in five; at University College London, more than 10% of international students are Chinese.

How did this happen? In part, the boom is due to the weak pound and America's trade war with China. Then there's the uncomfortable fact that a postgraduate degree in the UK is less competitive than those in China. An MA here typically lasts only a year, but brings in the lucrative fee of £30,000-plus in tuition alone. Undergraduates from non-EU countries pay triple the tuition fee, so it's easy to see why universities are taking fewer UK students each year and using foreign students to plug their funding gaps. With as many as 40% of Chinese students cancelling their plans to return to the UK in the fall, our universities – built by humble UK taxpayers – might spend more time on educating their home-grown students instead of hawking their degrees in the international marketplace.

As we wander into our tentative re-entry, Covid-19 is still unfolding as a morality tale of science, politics, economics and culture. Those of us who have emerged disease-free may feel like escape artists, but there is a limit to our recklessness. Sheltering in place for a long season has made us wary of change, made us yearn for the good old days when only bank robbers and surgeons wore masks, and we were unselfconscious innocents who could eat in restaurants, send children to school, go to church, see a film and use the loos in Peter Jones without feeling that the dice are loaded against us. Now we want to walk down familiar streets where everything looks exactly as we expected, only rather better.

Picking up where we left off is neither possible nor wise. If we are to deserve the world that awaits us, we will need imagination, generosity of spirit and audacity. I'd like to think this means ditching HS2 and using that money to pay the bills so the next generation isn't bled dry. That we will scrap the plans for Sizewell C. The technology is already out of date and the price tag more than £20 billion. We could use those billions to address the crisis in care homes and home care. A stark message of this pandemic is that how a society looks after its ageing population is a precise and sobering expression of its humanity.

Above all, we should now prepare for the next epidemics looming on the horizon. That doesn't mean 'every man for himself' and filling the cellar with loo paper, light bulbs and cases of Sauvignon Blanc. It means making those who govern the land know that we know they were not prepared this time. They did not understand the science, and their fear and confusion was as contagious as the alien virus.

Such chaos is not created in a day. It has long roots, and it begins with the belief 'it can't happen here'. We now know it can. We are not asleep and we are all changed. When we finally look back, we may realise it was in the twinkling of an eye.

July 7, 2020

WALKING IN THE WIND

IN this summer of 2020, I have whole days when I feel as if I'm living in a trance. I spend half the day preparing for the apocalypse of the second Covid-19 wave, and half looking after chickens, moving last year's ram lambs into fields with more grass and clearing out lean-tos on redundant farm buildings so that folks have somewhere to get out of the rain. In troubled times, you can justify your existence by simply shifting things around.

All the same, I get touchy when I open emails that start: 'How's life in the Wyken bubble?' I'm tempted to write back that this farm isn't surrounded by a sky-high fence that gives it immunity from a deadly virus, bypasses the plummeting economy and turns off *Today* with its reminders that the Government's understanding of what comes next is as tenuous as our own.

I don't snap back because, well, there is some truth to the 'bubble' thing. Country life still feels like a retreat, a kind of reprieve from the worst that can happen. Graphs show that fewer of us get coronavirus and, when we do, fewer of us die. Rural poverty is bleak, but it isn't crammed into tower blocks. Country children live in a safer world than city kids, and we like to believe that the country lanes protect them from the stench of racism, the reach of violence.

I thought of this a couple of weeks ago in the farmers' market as I walked behind a mother and daughter on their way to see the lambs. In her sundress, straw hat and wellies, the little girl had the purposeful stride of a country girl, kicking the gravel as she walked and talked.

'Why do they say black labs matter? Don't yellow labs matter?' 'They aren't saying "black *labs* matter", pumpkin. They're saying "black *lives* matter".' 'Why do they say that?' 'Because some black people have very difficult lives.' The little girl looked up at her mother. 'Where do the black lives live?' Under my mask, I stifled a smile, but I thought: 'Good question!'

Nowhere in the bustling market was a black face to be seen. When black faces do appear at the market or in the vineyard restaurant, they are usually from the American bases at Lakenheath and Mildenhall. The British countryside is a white world.

When you spend four months in one place without leaving, you start to chew over things. Anything can trigger it: the last of the peonies, the wishbone drying in the kitchen window. For me, it was the little girl's questions, questions that coincided with

158

news of the death of John Lewis in America. His was a life of dignity, grace and courage. A black life that mattered during the darkest days of America's past. The Civil Rights hero didn't die of Covid-19, he died of a fast-moving cancer, but that he lived to reach 80 was itself a miracle. The third of 10 children, the son of sharecroppers in Alabama, he was a country child in the segregated South, where black lives were never safe and faced a long struggle to prove they mattered.

On the day of Lewis's funeral, I walked down the drive to a farm cottage that houses a collection of books, photographs and papers on the Civil Rights movement in America. It seemed the right place to be. On the wall is a framed poster of a young Lewis kneeling with two others outside a segregated swimming pool in Cairo, Illinois, in 1962, shortly before his arrest. He was 22 years old, and it was half a century before sportsmen would 'take the knee'.

I took down his memoir, *Walking With The Wind*. The title came from his memory of crowding into a small wooden house with 15 of his cousins during a summer thunderstorm. The house began to shake and sway and planks of the wooden floor began to bend. The storm was pulling the house towards the sky. His aunt lined the children up and told them to hold hands. Throughout the storm, she guided them to the corners that were rising. As the wind shifted, so did the small cousins. The trembling house was held down by the weight of their small bodies.

That experience marked Lewis throughout his long life, a life shaped by listening to Martin Luther King's sermons on the radio as a young boy. He became a friend and a disciple of Dr King, and, despite more than 45 arrests and beatings, including a cracked skull when, aged 25, he led the march across the bridge in Selma, Lewis never wavered from his belief in non-violence. Even at his lowest, shattered by the assassinations of his two heroes, Dr King and Robert Kennedy, he held fast to his belief that, to keep the house from being pulled down, we have to hold hands and move together. He stood back from the increasing militancy and separatism that would doom the Civil Rights movement.

The cottage looks out on to the arable plains of East Anglia. It's a long way from the rural apartheid in the South of my childhood, where signs saying 'Colored' and 'White' were on water fountains and waiting-room doors. Thanks to the courage of people such as Lewis, those signs are history. But history can move forwards and backwards. I shared with Lewis the belief that President Obama's election meant that America had become a post-racial country. That optimism has evaporated with the present occupant of the White House.

I mourn a man whose moral compass always pointed in the right direction. It's not easy to see hope in these times of divisive rhetoric and partisanship but, like wishing on a wishbone, I look for signs. Three former presidents – one black, two white, one Republican, two Democrats – delivered stirring eulogies at the funeral of John Lewis. The weight of their words could save the trembling land in the storm that lies ahead.

I also find hope in a little girl who kicks the gravel as she strides forth. She's asking questions. She's not living in a bubble. Before you know it, this will be her world.

August 12, 2020

AN ALPHABET FOR UNCERTAIN TIMES

'ALL Property is Theft.' The French anarchist Proudhon's rallying cry hung on my wall in 1968. I'd now quite like a poster above the AGA that says: 'All property developers are thieves.'

BBC. To whom it may concern: faithful Radio 4 listeners (average age 56) turn off the radio when the comedy programmes come on at 6.30pm and 11pm. Segregation of the airways based on sensitivity and intelligence is perfectly acceptable – I think you'll find that Trollope and Julian Barnes rarely appear on Radio 1.

COUNTRY LIFE is a weekly periodical with a surprisingly diverse, literate, open-minded and prescient readership.

'DÉJÀ VU all over again', first uttered by Yogi Berra, expresses how we feel when we hear the words 'Brexit', 'deal or no deal' and politicians on Radio 4's *Today*.

ENGLISHMEN are much admired in the Deep South. My grandmother always regretted that I was headstrong and farouche, but when I married an Englishman she changed her will and left me the family silver.

FARMERS are noble custodians of the countryside and salt of the earth, until they are offered £5 million for nine acres where 250 houses will be built. Upon completion, the farmer will move to the Dordogne with his new wife.

GOOGLE is 22 years old this year, but I can't remember life before Google. Question: is Google the life raft of the forgetful or are our memories shot because of the propinquity of Google?

'HOPE is the thing with feathers.' I, too, love Emily Dickinson, but most of us need more substantial signs of hope: a clean bill of health, a tax refund, banana bread.

IN uncertain times, only one thing is certain: almost everything will work again if you unplug it for three minutes.

JERUSALEM and *Land of Hope and Glory* are the soundtracks to our pilgrimage to a place we heard of long ago. The music is in our bones, and we know most of the words.

KINDNESS is everything. If I see someone being unkind – to a waiter, a dog, a child, a partner – I never forget it. It's useful to remember that when I am feeling unkind.

LIES told by children are mischievous and inventive. Lies told by political leaders dehumanise all who believe them.

MONEY. All Jane Austen's first paragraphs – indeed, first lines – include money. Love only comes into the story later. The English would rather disclose their weight than their bank balance. The only rule is not to talk about money with those who have much more or much less than you.

'NOTHING terrible lasts forever.' Wise words from my Hungarian friend George Lang, who survived both Nazi and Russian prison camps. He made it to New York in the 1950s, where he revived the famous Café des Artistes. He died aged 86, proof that, in fact, nothing lasts forever.

OLD AGE comes as a slow and outlandish surprise. Fortunately, it's a number that benefits from constant revision.

PARKER MORRIS standards established the

minimum space in dwellings needed for human happiness. He also required all rooms to be heated and all homes to have storage. His gift to humanity was rewarded with a knighthood, but the rules were abolished in 1980. If I could change one thing...

QUEEN ELIZABETH II will be a hard act to follow, but this country is lucky to have The Prince of Wales. He's been right about architecture, organic tomatoes and the planet. He also has very nice clothes.

RITUALS – weddings, christenings, handshakes, coronations – give structure to life. Of all the rituals coronavirus has deprived us of, the one I miss most is the funeral, the sacrament of tender farewell that underlines the preciousness and mystery of life.

SIZEWELL C has gone from £14 billion costs to £20 billion before it's even begun. The nuclear-power scheme by French energy giant EDF and the state-owned Chinese CGN has tripled in size and cost and will carve up ancient woodland, farms, rural communities and a fragile heritage coast. Idea: instead of raising taxes to get the country out of our economic hole, cancel Sizewell.

TEETH become more relevant every year of your life. Your front teeth are only as healthy as your back teeth.

UBIQUITOUS is a word that should be used sparingly. Ditto Unprecedented.

VIGOROUS writing is concise. Believe it or not.

WOMAN. Until recently, this was not a controversial word, but I'm with J. K. Rowling on this. I know all the words to Tammy Wynette's *Stand by your Man*: 'Sometimes it's hard to be a woman.'

X is the Greek letter for Chi, which is the first letter for the word Christ. There is no excuse for writing Xmas to save time.

YEATS'S poem *Responsibilities* has the epitaph 'In dreams begin responsibilities'. Is it an epigram or an aphorism? Google it.

ZOOM meetings have convinced a whole generation they can live in the country and gaze at sheep as they run the world from their barn conversion. I think they'll find it's a bit more complicated than that.

September 9, 2020

LETTER TO AMERICA

SOMETIMES an event so dramatic occurs that time seems to stand still – a wildfire, a catastrophic flood, tanks rolling down the tree-lined avenue of a capital city. You may think me feeble, but the presidential debate in Ohio on October 1 felt like one of those cataclysmic events. You may say, 'but nobody got hurt. Nobody died.' But I'm not sure. In my rather long life, I've never witnessed a president behave as I saw that evening. Not for the first time in nearly four years, I believed that this US President has done irremediable harm to American democracy.

I said, 'in my rather long life'. So, how old am I? Well, I'm younger than either of the men running for President, but older than the last one. In fact, I'm the age of the woman who ran four years ago, the one who got nearly three million more popular votes than Donald Trump, but lost in the democratic mirage known as the Electoral College: Trump 304; Hillary Clinton 227.

I'm also old enough to have watched the first televised presidential debate: Kennedy versus Nixon. On the evening of September 26, 1960, our family sat in front of our black-and-white television. I suspect my parents each had a bourbon and water; my sister and I had mugs of Ovaltine.

What I remember: Kennedy, at 43, looked young and handsome – I would even say he appeared urbane, telegenic and presidential, but those words were not in my vocabulary; Nixon, only four years older, looked tired, unhappy and not youthful. Not a good look for someone who wants to be president.

Years later, we learned how Kennedy had prepared. For days, he practised in mock debates. He chose a dark-blue suit so he would stand out against the drab studio walls. On the afternoon of the debate, he relaxed on the hotel roof, studied his notes, worked on his tan and listened to Peggy Lee records. Later, his own make-up artist applied the right stuff for the bright studio lights.

Nixon, recently out of hospital with an inflamed knee, spent the afternoon delivering a speech to the Chicago Carpenters Union. When he arrived at the TV station, he banged his bad knee on the car door. His light-grey suit blended with the bland walls, he rejected the offer of make-up that might have disguised his five o'clock shadow. The debate was the turning point in the election that Kennedy won by only 112,827 votes.

It would be 16 years before Americans saw another televised presidential debate. By the time Gerald Ford debated the Georgia peanut farmer Jimmy Carter in 1976, the electorate was worn out. The war in Vietnam had ended, and the US had lost. Watergate was over, and Nixon had departed the White House in disgrace. If anyone now remembers that debate, it's because Ford claimed: 'There is no Soviet domination of Eastern Europe.' The incredulous moderator, mentioning Poland, Romania and Yugoslavia, gave him the chance to rephrase the statement, but Ford stuck to his guns – and lost the election. Those were the days when fact-checking mattered.

If the Ford-Carter debate has faded from memory, the Trump-Biden debate in Ohio will live forever in cyberspace. Generations will be able to watch the US President as the aggressive and cruel school bully who beats up every kid in the playground. Whenever the teacher/moderator tries to stop him, the bully kicks him.

They will see the honourable Mr Biden as a conscientious objector dodging bullets on the battlefield as he rescues the fallen. Even when he says something important, his words are lost in the crossfire. But when the polls – and a number of significant Republicans – call Mr Biden the 'winner', I don't agree. The debate was like a Tarantino film where no one wins. It was a spectacular loss for American democracy.

It may already be forgotten. As the millions who watched the Trump-Biden debate were still experiencing aftershocks, another event occurred, a radical denouement worthy of an Oscar: the President and First Lady had tested positive for coronavirus, the disease that the President first denied and then failed to contain as he taunted citizens who wore masks, belittled doctors, ignored scientists, claimed hydroxychloroquine would protect him, and told his country, where more than

200,000 people have died of it: 'Don't be afraid of Covid, Don't let it dominate your life.' Lord have mercy.

Still, Covid-19 is not something even I would wish on my worst enemy. Honest. I have never pronounced *Schadenfreude* with confidence, and I worry that 'poetic justice' could backfire. I genuinely want President Trump to recover because I want America to have a fair and honest election with a decisive public vote that restores a more uplifting vision of democracy, preferably one where billionaires pay more tax than hairdressers, and honesty, dignity, competence, decency and eloquence are valued.

I'm lucky to be old enough to remember a president who said: 'A strong nation, like a strong person, can afford to be gentle, firm, thoughtful, and restrained. It can afford to extend a helping hand to others. It is a weak nation, like a weak person, that must behave with bluster and boasting and rashness and other signs of insecurity.' (President Carter.)

I'm also old enough to admit I'd really like an election in which the candidates are younger than I am. I am amazed that this is a battle between two old men. My English husband reminds me that Churchill formed his last ministry in his 77th year, but I'm not reassured. When Mr Trump and Mr Biden speak, I think of Benjamin Franklin's 'By my rambling digressions I perceive myself to be growing old'. I could add 'ditto'.

October 14, 2020

LONG DAY'S JOURNEY INTO
THE WILD BLUE YONDER

I AM writing this at the kitchen table. The soundtrack in my head is Dolly Parton singing *What Ain't To Be Just Might Happen*. The background noise in the room is *Today* on Radio 4 with Jon Sopel telling me what I already know: that America may – or may not – have four more years of Donald Trump. That the melodramatic story is not over.

I'm 3,000 miles or so from Dollywood outside of Nashville, on a farm in Suffolk, nine miles from the sugar-beet factory in Bury St Edmunds. Last night, as I waited for Katty Kay and Christian Fraser to begin the BBC's coverage of the election, my fellow Americans were still standing in lines that stretch nearly as far as the beet factory to cast their vote for the next President of the United States.

What with the long lines of voters and publishing deadlines, I am writing this without knowing who is going to win. You have an advantage: barring stomping, tweeting and – new word for me – lawyer'ng, when you read this you will know who's going to occupy the White House for the next four years.

Not knowing makes me sick with anxiety but there is something worse: it is knowing that America is in such a dark place. Each side in this election believes that the victory of the other will bring about the end of their country as they know it. All the citizens of that vast and rich land believe the country they love is doomed if one half of it – the 'other' half – is victorious. The partisanship is so profound that when you hear the refrain of 'lies, lies, lies!' it could be a reporter on CNN railing against a President known to be a braggart, a bully and a liar. Or it could be the angry voice of Fox News, accusing the Biden team and the 'liberal media' of 'lies, lies, lies!'.

This is not a battle between two political parties, an ideological contest or a culture war. It's like a religious war, with no forgiveness in sight.

Our patch of East Anglia, 45 minutes from Lakenheath and Mildenhall, two of America's main air bases in Britain, is like a field of dreams. I figure that about half of the Americans who come to the farmers' market each Saturday, or eat in the vineyard restaurant, are Trump supporters. Divisions and differences that have scarred their friends and families back home – economic, medical, political, racial – are on hold on these air bases, model villages of an idealised America where every need is met and discipline is enforced. The Stars and Stripes flies high over the amber waves of grain that are pure Suffolk.

It's very different for my friends who live in Trumpland America, where Covid-19 and economic disaster are surging, masks are a political statement and 'right to carry' laws permit you to take your gun to the grocery store, the bar, to church, even to hospital should you have trouble breathing. The 'right' to carry a gun is considered as fundamental a right as liberty and the pursuit of happiness.

My friend Mac Gordon, a fearless reporter who lives in rural Georgia, writes about armed militia groups patrolling the streets in some American towns and cities. I look at these armed men with assault rifles in Charlottesville, Portland and Seattle from my position of safety in front of a slender television screen. The reality is terrifying.

Mac also has a sound track for these times. His is a mournful old country song by Porter Wagoner: *I've Enjoyed as Much of This as I Can Stand*. He reckons that the title is how most Americans feel about the past four years, wherever they stand. Mac and I were both born and raised in the South, so we know in our bones how long divisions can persist. So much has been stripped and laid bare by these past four years that it's hard to believe we're going to see an end in our lifetime. Once the populist fervour is unleashed, it's hard to get it back into the bottle.

As I was writing this column, Mr Trump declared

that he'd won. Never mind that millions of postal votes were yet to be counted, he called for the counting to stop and for the Supreme Court to get ready. He wants to fight it out.

If you are worried about your job, or affordable health care, or climate change, guns, opioid deaths, coronavirus, moral character or the education of your children – all the things Americans put on their list of worries – those will have to wait. The first email to arrive in my inbox is brief: We are living under the volcano.

In the peace and warmth of my kitchen, I look out on to the apple orchard where chickens and peacocks check out the windfalls. The dog at my feet snores softly. On the wall by the window hangs a slate plaque carved with the words that hung over Karl Jung's front door: *Bidden or not bidden, God is present*. The words have a theological suppleness that comforts me.

One morning, I had one of those hazy moments when I thought it said 'Biden or not Biden, God is present'. By the time you read this, America – and the world – will know: Biden or not Biden. God only knows – and I hope He is present.

November 11, 2020

HAPHAZARD BY STARLIGHT

ADVENT is a time of waiting, and we have become a congregation of experts. I nominate the people of Planet Earth for the Nobel Prize for Waiting. Even in a country smaller than Montana, we have modified our motto 'Keep Calm and Carry On' to 'Keep Waiting and Stay Home'.

We have waited for Brexit negotiators to come up with a deal, for test and trace to slow down the virus, and waited for schools, theatres, restaurants and shops to re-open. Then, after they opened and closed again, with stoic hearts we began another wait. We've waited for reunions with our loved ones and old friends and, with hope against hope, we have waited for a miracle: a vaccine to save us from a deadly virus.

Even now that hope has arrived and we are free to acquire the inessential things in life, still we wait, for dental appointments and for deliveries from Amazon and AbeBooks, Holland & Barrett and John Lewis. We've replaced the urge to wander with the urge to order. It's worse for my American family who are waiting for Donald Trump to leave the White House.

'We are living in the last act of a play by Shakespeare,' writes my cousin Marguerite in Tennessee. 'We expected it to be bad, but we didn't expect it to be worse than we expected.'

On the chimneypiece, invitations to weddings that didn't take place are now joined by Christmas cards. With heavy hearts, we wait for dates for memorial services, gatherings that assuage the grief and comfort the spirit in a way the services confined to six people last spring cannot achieve. 2020 has been like a run of *Waiting for Godot*. Remember the two men sitting on the park bench? One says: 'Let's go.' The other says: 'We can't.' 'Why not?' 'We're waiting for Godot.'

I first saw the play in a small town in rural Mississippi when it was performed by the Free Southern Theatre, a troupe of travelling actors touring the South in the summer of 1964. It was before the Voting Rights Act, and members of the black community had waited 100 years for their right to vote. Theirs was a vocation of waiting: waiting for decent schools and hospitals, waiting for a seat on the bus. They'd never heard of an Irish playwright called Samuel Beckett (neither had I), but they knew about staying in place, knew the feeling of being worn out from waiting.

Godot never turns up, but it turned out better in the South. A Voting Rights Act was passed, but no one could say that the waiting ended. Things were better in Advent: a child was born and the world got Christmas, but the days ahead were hardly smooth sailing. The arrival of the vaccine feels like a modern-day miracle, but scientists and doctors predict that we will still be in masks and 'social distancing' for another year.

I love the sublime Advent collect in which we entreat God to 'give us grace that we may cast away the works of darkness, and put upon us the armour of light, now in the time of this mortal life'. The vaccine feels like an armour of light, arriving in the nick of time in this mortal life, even as today's wise men and women try to tell us that our period of waiting is not over.

I understand why people haven't felt like waiting this Christmas. I used to be quite 'high church' about not bringing it into the house before December 20, but not this year. I went through old CDs in search of Joan Baez's *Noël* and Elvis's *I'll be Home for Christmas*, *The John Rutter Christmas Album* and Carols from King's, my playlist for putting out my crèche collection. It's a ceremony that usually takes several hours and a couple of glasses of eggnog. This year, I did it in a morning with a pot of coffee. I couldn't wait.

When I tell people that our son, Sam, and his wife, Georgia, will be with her family this year, I see a look of sadness in their eyes. I'm surprised because the Christmas in 'Tiers' has re-written a lot of plans. I believe the rota should not be fixed in stone and 'Home for Christmas' changes over the years. I also like the idea of a Christmas morning that begins with the two of us feeding the Shetland sheep and four new pigs. I will console my chickens and ancient turkeys, baffled by their confinement due to avian flu, with their favourite food: warm porridge. It feels timeless and sacred to begin Christmas Day in the company of animals and the smell of hay.

For my first Christmas presiding over a full house of new in-laws, my sister sent me an apron she had made from cranberry-red velvet. In its original version it was the dress I wore as bridesmaid at her first wedding, a Christmas wedding. Christmas is a tricky time to get married, and that marriage unravelled like velvet cut on the bias, but the dress has now had three decades as a festive apron. In thread of holly green, she embroidered the words 'The Christmas Martyr'.

This year, no martyrdom is required. There is no stockpile of food, no endless meals, no schedule that requires the timing of a production of *Aida*. All we need are a few delicacies – a goose for two – and rare bottles of wine that are best drunk *à deux*. There will be time to sit and wonder, to savour the memories of Christmases past.

In the attic next to three generations of decorations is a box of books that comes out for a month each year: anthologies of Yuletide stories, Elizabeth David's *Christmas*, Christmas poems, several editions of *Christmas with the Savages*, a dozen of the *Christmas Crackers* produced each year by John Julius Norwich and a much-loved volume by the poet U. A. Fanthorpe, who wrote a poem each year to send with her cards. Each one has a Quaker brevity; a favourite is *BC:AD*, about the birth of Jesus. It ends:

> And this was the moment
> When a few farm workers and three
> Members of an obscure Persian sect
> Walked haphazard by starlight straight
> Into the kingdom of heaven.

I pray the year ahead will not be as haphazard as the year past, that the days ahead will be lit by starlight. I can't wait.

December 16, 2020

V

*I've Enjoyed As Much Of This
As I Can Stand*

SINGING IN THE TURNIP FIELDS
OF HOPE

WHEN the miracle arrived, I didn't fall to my knees in prayerful gratitude. In my bewildered and relieved state, I burst into song: 'Vaccine! Vaccine! Vaccine! *Vaccine*! Please take away this plague!' My lyrics didn't stretch beyond two lines, but I belted them out to the stunned audience of sheep munching on turnip greens. My improvised version of Dolly Parton's *Jolene*, a song that's made her millions, felt good because the singer gave a big wad of those millions to Vanderbilt University in Nashville to fund vaccine research.

Singing in a field of turnips requires as much stamina as clinging on to hope. When I'm breathless and out of tune, I hush for a while and work on my Gratitude lists. 'Vaccine' is at the top, but 'Deal' and 'Biden and Harris' are close behind. However doomed life looks (did I say that I'm writing this in lockdown number three with 40 staff back on furlough and after the worst year on the farm in living memory?),

I remind myself that 2021 could have started with the re-election of Trump, the stormy chaos of no deal – and no vaccine.

My concentration is shot, but I try to keep those things in mind. I believe that one of the unrecognised aspects of this strange, uncertain time is a kind of universal Attention Deficit Disorder. No data is available, but this distraction permeates the atmosphere like an invisible ash cloud. I go from room to room, never quite sure what I'm searching for. I put a load in the washing machine, but it lingers there, unwashed and unmissed. Cards that were written and stamped spent Christmas in a Daunt book bag on the floor of the larder.

More alarming (make that irritating), a random word can send me on a journey. When my husband announced in solemn voice that 'the Oxford vaccine is the lifeboat that will return us to normal life', I launched into a story about Hélène, the cook and *femme de ménage* who ran the rue de Fleurus household for Gertrude Stein and Alice B. Toklas. When *Titanic* sank, Hélène said she thought that the Anglo-Saxon gallantry of women and children first was unintelligent and unnatural. What was the point of a bunch of widows without husbands to take care of them? Who, indeed, would row the lifeboat?

My husband's eyes glazed over halfway through that philosophical slingshot before I got to my point: speaking of lifeboats, who should get the vaccine first? In the practical voice of Hélène, I questioned the intelligence of starting with the longest living. For one thing, they're the ones most likely to stay put. In the early days of Covid-19, elderly patients were pushed out of hospitals and put into care homes where they died in large numbers. In our ignorance, we behaved like a country of brutes and barbarians. Remorse for that tragedy led to over-eighties first.

Making these life-and-death decisions requires skill on a par with smashing atoms. It shouldn't be left to politicians, but to those rare souls who are wise and brave and good and know something about the behaviour of viruses. I'm in favour of scientists who are dedicated to the truth.

My list puts doctors, nurses and all hospital staff at the top. I'd keep the 'vulnerable' and their carers up there (callous and heartless I am not), followed by dentists, teachers, bus and train drivers, police, firemen and the military. Also high up would be post-office staff and delivery folk; builders and repairmen; vets; clergy of all faiths so they can keep consoling their flocks; farmers, for the same reason; MPs (not so high – we should have virtual sittings until Covid-19 is gone), but prison officers, guards and prisoners can't operate virtually. And the 50-somethings who are looking after their 80-something parents. As the practical French cook knew: until there are enough lifeboats for everyone, you have to start with the rowers.

I confess that many of the people I love most would be lopped off the top of my list. Some agree with me and are embarrassed at being a priority. Others do not and are complaining about the delay for the second vaccine. The young who inhabit this patch don't question the distribution order. They are more concerned about the changing of the world order as they watch global warming edging ever closer to 1.5°C and wildfires consuming Portugal, Australia, Brazil and the west coast of America. They are also paying the costs: deferred exams, deferred careers and deferred dreams.

Meanwhile, we do the best we can. In 30 years of married life, I rarely had a morning when I went downstairs, made coffee and returned to bed with mug and book. I now plan to do it once a week and, if his paws aren't wet with dew, the dog comes too.

Coffee, dogs and books feed the soul. I'm planning to get to the new John Grisham as soon as I finish the book I'm reading. You might think *The Great Influenza: The Story of the Deadliest Pandemic in History* by John M. Barry is not a book to read during a pandemic. Perhaps you don't want to know about the virus that erupted in an army camp in Kansas in 1918, killing more people in 24 weeks than AIDS killed in 24 years, and more in a year than the Black Death killed in a century. You'd be wrong. When it was published in 2004, it was seen as the masterful, compelling template for confronting the epidemics that loomed on the horizon.

Somewhere along the way, the people who make decisions about our world got distracted. They stopped paying attention. They stopped investing in lifeboats. I reckon if they had read Mr Barry's book I wouldn't be writing this in lockdown and you might be reading *Country Life* in front of a blazing fire in a country inn. May we all pay attention in 2021.

January 13, 2021

LIFE AND DEATH IN THE AGE OF 'AT LEAST'

IT'S the middle of the afternoon and we are in the kitchen eating sweet-potato soup and cornbread. There's also a bottle of Sancerre on the table. Wine with soup is confusing, but the occasion called for more than soup on its own. This is a wake. There are only the two of us, so it is lawful, a husband-and-wife bubble that has returned home from the funeral of the husband's oldest friend.

No, the friend did not die of Covid-19. I'm telling you that right away because that's what everyone wants to know. It's the look you see in eyes peering over the mask when you break the news, the look in your eyes when you hear the news. It's the haiku at the end of the obituary: age and cause of death. When the age is advanced, a silent sigh descends. When the cause is 'undisclosed', a small shiver, the word 'Covid' a tremor.

For years, I saved the obituaries until last. Leaving

behind the world at war, crime, MeToo, drugs, fraud, injustice, soil erosion and obesity, I'd pour a second cup of coffee and enter a small oasis of calm. Touching, intriguing, mostly devoid of sentimentality and mostly beautifully written, these are the true novellas about a world in which people with sad beginnings did remarkable things and people with remarkable beginnings lost the lucky pass they received at birth and went the wrong way. I did not read and weep. Instead I read and marvelled.

Life in a pandemic has changed everything. Covid-19 has turned poets into actuaries and the numbers overwhelm us. Daily, we are told how many tested positive in the past 24 hours, how many died after testing positive, the spiral descending like a snowstorm. Then there is light in the dark, the news is revealed in percentages. Spring may bring fritillaries, but new numbers will burst forth: the survival rates of the vaccinated according to race, age and pharmaceutical origin.

Statistics may be food for thought for the epidemiologists, but they do not provide the benison of understanding required by less numerate mortals. We want to know the details of dying. Like moths to a flame, we are lured to the hidden secrets of life's ending. I used to think it was a Southern thing, the birthright of those born in the land of Faulkner and Flannery O'Connor and layaway funeral plans. Only after I left the melancholy Kudzu hills did

I understand that death and dying is not a regional obsession. It is the essential truth of humanity. Look at the pictures: all Christian art is divided between birth – baby Jesus on His mother's lap – and death, the Cross giving the Christian faith its evocative symbol. *Ars moriendi*, indeed, and, you could say, the most powerful logo ever devised by Man.

Christoph, short for Christopher, celebrated his birthday on a sunny October day. Lunch was a conscientiously distanced party of six. We ate his favourite food – Stoberry potted shrimps – and toasted the birthday boy. Two newish hips meant that, in his eightieth year, he had the vigour of a 50-year-old, striding across fields with the young dog and the old dog. The saying that 'Age is psychological, not chronological' isn't true: it's physiological. He who strides forth drinks from the fountain of youth and remains buoyant. Christoph relished the company of his five children and their families, confessing that the spring lockdown had been a gift: he'd loved having them living in the house, spending rare and precious time with them, especially the youngest ones: 'In real life it would never have happened.'

It was in that mood of confident optimism that, on the second day of January, his wife drove him to Papworth for a stent to be inserted in a clogged artery. Once there, the doctors decided to delay the stent and continue to treat the problem with drugs. Christoph went home and enjoyed the unexpected dinner with his wife and daughter. The next morning he had a heart attack and died.

Those are the details that got us here. The limited congregation included his three brothers and a covey of lifelong friends, all of whom qualify for the first rung of the vaccine. Their words were muffled by masks, but sounded like a distant Greek chorus.

'At least he didn't get Covid.'
'At least he didn't spend two months on a ventilator.'
'At least he didn't get Alzheimer's.'
'At least he didn't have a stroke.'

We have entered the Age of At Least.

The days are getting longer, but it's growing dark in the kitchen and the Sancerre is warm. This is not a wake, it's a cameo of a wake, but it punctuates the day, provides us with a little more time to remember wild adventures, to give thanks for the man who gave our five-year-old son the fishing lesson one summer at Garynahine that shaped the direction of his life.

I ask for one more telling of the story of Christoph, aged 16, the only member of the trio to bag three geese on a wildfowling trip. The daylight retrieve revealed his geese to be a seagull, a shelduck and a barn owl. My husband likes to think that remorse for his ill-fated quarry turned his friend into a serious ornithologist.

Some day we will look back on this in bewilderment. Will anyone believe that the only gatherings permitted were funerals and that those were limited? Will we admit the no-singing rule rather improved the service, especially when the hymns were sung by the choir of King's College, Cambridge and the sound system was state of the art?

What we missed most was the wake: the rare gathering of old friends, the chance to hold on a little longer to the life that has gone and the telling of the old stories when life was so much fun.

February 10, 2021

PARIS WAS YESTERDAY

THE lane between the farm and the village was still half underwater, so my husband, jabbed weeks ago, insisted on driving me to the village hall in his pickup truck. We loaded up like an old couple going on a day trip to the seaside, me with a Thermos of coffee, an extra wool scarf and a stack of Robin Lane Fox's columns from the weekend *FT*, my husband with *Times 2* and David McCullough's hefty life of Harry Truman. The dog jumped in the back seat.

Five minutes later, I walked straight in, handed over my form, and was directed to my GP. I never even felt the 'slight sting' he warned me about. Heading towards the exit, I saw a dozen or so people sitting in metal chairs, well spaced out. Silent and pale-faced behind their masks, they looked more like prisoners awaiting trial than giddy pensioners on the road to liberation. Only when my husband, looking up from the crossword, asked 'why are you back so soon?', did I realise my fellow citizens were following instructions to wait 15 minutes in case of a reaction.

And, 10 minutes later, I did have a reaction. Not one connected to AstraZeneca, but an eerie swoop of *déjà vu*. The scene of the subdued villagers took me back to the Préfecture de Police on the Île de la Cité in Paris, waiting for my *carte de séjour* to be renewed. That, too, was a room filled with apprehension – and mostly Algerians, Moroccans, Turks and Yugoslavs.

We sat in silence, clutching our numbered tickets, our bundles of papers with elaborate stamps and signatures, and our passports. Because the French regard all foreigners as criminals, the room had the stench of guilt. We all wanted the same thing: another stamp and the benediction of inexplicable French bureaucracy.

My post-jab *souvenir du temps perdu* did not come out of the blue. After a lockdown year of mostly harmonious marital togetherness watching re-runs of *Dad's Army*, *Vera*, *Poirot* and *Midsomer Murders*, I have crossed the channel. I have defected and am back in Paris. Not Netflix's *Emily in Paris* (if desperate, I'll try again), but *Call My Agent!*, the French series on Netflix. And *Lupin*, the fast-paced series based on the gentleman burglar. The scenes of Paris are sensational, and make me long to wander into a cafe and mutter: '*Un verre de Saint-Amour, s'il vous plaît.*'

I know my days of walking across the Pont Alexandre III, my precious *carte de séjour* safely tucked in my shoulder bag at all times (the French accept identity cards as a privilege of *civilisation*), won't return but, after a year of pastoral life in the company of DCI Vera Stanhope, I dream of surly waiters, terrifying taxi drivers and impatient shopkeepers from the Auvergne who correct my French as I pay for my *jambon*.

It doesn't take much to send me into a French reverie. My Suffolk kitchen is a museum of treasures from the Porte de Vanves flea market, a five-minute journey on my VéloSolex from my tiny *atelier* in the 14th: Grey Poupon mustard jars, bowls from Vallauris, *marché* signs for *l'escargots* in *vieilles francs*, things that now cost a fortune on Etsy. Above my desk is a photograph of Ernest Hemingway and Janet Flanner drinking cognac in the Deux Magots in 1945.

The two writers were members of the expatriate community that arrived in Paris in the 1920s. Hemingway was the best known as *The Sun Also Rises* had been published in New York. Flanner's fame came later from her fortnightly 'Letter from Paris', which appeared in *The New Yorker* for 30 years. Her long career ended just as I arrived in Paris, but an early collection of those 'Letters', the slender volume *Paris Was Yesterday*, was my bible, my guide to the city and to all things French.

Flanner said that *Paris Was Yesterday* made no sense as a title, that the publishers chose it because it was 'provocative'. If she were alive now, she might find the title poetic and apt. Her Paris (1925-75) is not the Paris of today; it is not my Paris (1975-81). The skyscrapers in La Défense could be Hong Kong, the Portuguese concierges have been replaced by panels with codes for the residents. The Yugoslav factory workers have gone back to their villages because the factories have gone and so has Yugoslavia.

It's not even the Paris of the addictive Netflix films. Those films were made *sans* masks, *sans* curfews, *sans* lockdown. Paris now shuts down from 6pm to 6am. Masks are compulsory from the age of six (homemade masks not allowed). A naked face will get you a fine of €135.

Writing on December 7, 1940, Flanner called her Letter *Paris, Germany*. 'Paris is now the capital of limbo,' she began. 'Anybody who loved Paris and grieves at its plight is fortunate not to see it now.' No one would compare a pandemic and a lockdown to Occupied France, but anyone who loves the City of Light grieves at its plight. Just, it must be said, as one grieves at the plight of London and New York. Close the restaurants and cafes; shut the museums, theatres and cinemas; close shops (the shops!); reduce trains, buses and offices; remove children and noise, and the city becomes a lost civilisation, a memory of a time and place.

I still remember Flanner's beginning of *Paris Was Yesterday*: 'Memories are the specific invisible remains in our lives of what belongs in the past tense.' I have spent an entire year on a farm in Suffolk from which I have not strayed further than the post office in Stanton, the village shop in Ixworth, the vet in Bressingham and two funerals. I know I am lucky: the news is full of people trapped in cities, longing for fields and space. But there is magic in balance, and I pray for cities to come back to life. I dream of the day I go on the Eurostar, not forgetting that glamorous St Pancras is infinitely nicer than gloomy Gare du Nord. I long for the cities I love to emerge from the past tense.

March 10, 2021

THE HAPPINESS COURSE

JUST as Family and Friends Divided had become Friends Reunited, and the wretched Trump era laid to rest, Harry and Meghan gave their Oprah interview and a whole new Grand Canyon opened up again. This chasm really surprised me because my team was astonished to discover that I wasn't on the Sussexes' side.

I swear I did not come across all Piers Morgan. I didn't say: 'That was performance art, staged by two millionaires and a billionaire.' But, even as I tried to exercise restraint, I could hear the disappointment flowing through the cables that lie under the ocean that separates us.

When I protested that the Archbishop doesn't marry folks in his backyard, you'd have thought I'd become a Covid-19 denier. When I reckoned it was probably a spunky younger cousin who told Harry that she 'sure hopes your babies dilute the Spencer Ginger gene', nobody laughed. When it emerged the '*Whoa!*' fireball of the interview was made to Harry *before* they were married, I didn't bother to send an email. If there is one thing I have learned in life it is this: just let go.

I have been practising letting go a lot lately. In my family, we call it 'the politics of shutting up'. It's fine to be wise and sage about what matters in life, but the truth is that the way to happiness is to shut up and move on.

Happily, it turns out that it's never too late to be happy. Happiness can be learned, and nearly four million people have taken the Yale Happiness class since it became available online. In these times of trembling uncertainty, it felt like a good idea to check it out.

I didn't get very far. The 10-week online course is free if you are only grazing, and £35 if you want a 'Certificate'. Now called The Science of Well-Being, its weekly sessions have titles: 'Misconceptions About Happiness', 'Why Our Expectations Are So Bad', 'How Can We Overcome Our Biases'. The session 'Stuff That Really Makes Us Happy' was tempting because I've always found that stuff – books, pictures, nice sheets, *batterie de cuisine*, Roberts radios, goose-down pillows and navy cashmere turtlenecks – makes me really happy. Unfortunately, the 'Stuff' course is two hours long, plus written assignments, and I was afraid the stuff would be birdsong and oak leaves and forgiveness. All of which make me happy, but I'm uneasy when Nature is presented as a revelation and cure. Don't we all know that?

I went on to Google to see if there was a shorter version, which was a good move. It turns out that the road to happiness boils down to five words: sleep, gratitude and helping others.

The importance of sleep is not new to me. I read Matthew Walker's *Why We Sleep*, and it was life-changing. I still drink coffee and wine, but once you read that every major disease in the developed world – Alzheimer's, cancer, obesity, diabetes – has strong causal links to deficient sleep, you take to the bed. I may read Chips Channon's diaries until 1am, but I never take my laptop to bed. I no longer rely on the war-torn, climate-disaster tragedies of the World Service to keep me company on sleepless nights.

It sounds obvious, but the next best thing to sleep is gratitude. It is surprisingly easy to forget. The Happiness Course recommends that you keep a Gratitude Journal. Years ago, when Amazon was a 'good thing', I ordered a book on the Amish. I knew the wrong book had arrived as soon as I read on the cover 'phenomenal international bestseller – more than two million copies sold'. Because returns are an ordeal, I read *Simple Abundance* anyway. I squirmed when the writer told the reader to keep a Gratitude Journal, but I actually did it for a few months and, like Scott Fitzgerald making lists in *The Crack-up*, I suddenly felt better. So good I stopped writing.

I've never written more than 20 pages in a journal, but when I come across that pocket-size book now

I gratefully read a few pages. It's like finding a photograph of your younger self, and remembering when you had thicker hair and whiter teeth. Hokey as it sounds, scribbling a few things you are grateful for each night is a great sleep aid. It helps you make sense of your life, even if it's three words on the back of an envelope: goosedown pillow, vaccine, good dog. Chewing over things that you regret or resent is like drinking a double espresso before bedtime and planting the seeds of dementia.

The third way to maintaining optimism about the human condition is the most gallant: helping others. Here, I hit a certain lull. My husband believes everyone thinks they have a good sense of humour and that they are a good judge of character. I would add that most people think they help others. This is untrue. Clapping for the NHS and painting rainbows may feel like helping, but it isn't the same as creating a fund so that nurses who work a night shift get a free taxi home. Taking five bags of clothes to Oxfam feels like helping others, but you've really brought peace and happiness to yourself. Helping others is listening to someone who is lonely talk your ear off. It's buying lavish groceries for a person who has hit hard times instead of buying them for yourself. In the age of Covid-19, helping others is more complicated and more necessary than ever.

Which brings me back to Harry and Meghan. I tell my sister that they don't look happy. 'I don't think you can be the judge of that,' she says. I suspect that Harry rarely sees *Country Life* these days, but, if he does, I hope he will check out the Happiness Course. I'd also advise a Gratitude Journal.

Now that I've got that out of my system, I'm going to move on and work on the shutting-up thing. I have a new journal, which I have inscribed with a quote from my favourite 19th-century wit, Sydney Smith: 'We know nothing of tomorrow; our business is to be good and happy today.' My sister says that if I really do practise shutting up, she will start a Gratitude Journal and put my vow on the opening page. Before I do anything rash, however, I'll sleep on it.

April 14, 2021

TO HAVE AND TO HOLD

ON that muggy July afternoon when we stood in the chapel of the Palace of Westminster and vowed 'for better and for worse', 'in sickness and in health', I had never heard of hip replacements. Even heart bypasses were not well known – two decades would pass before Bill Clinton had one (four, actually), a surgical miracle presented as deliverance for a man with a family history of heart disease, a lifetime spent as a cigar-smoking workaholic with a passion for junk food, among other things.

I made those vows in innocence and ignorance. Despite my husband's belief that, in his experience (two new hips and a triple bypass), I'm a better consultant than nurse, I think I've honoured the 'sickness and health' thing with fortitude and grace. The one thing that never entered my head when we repeated those extravagant and ancient promises was a year of enforced togetherness: a quarantine duet, incarceration *à deux*, for better and for worse.

In the beginning, it felt like a second honeymoon. We had candlelit suppers, asparagus and crab linguini, bottles of Saint-Véran instead of Wyken wine. On our anniversary, I made the flourless Ottolenghi chocolate cake to have with our raspberries. More than once I said 'I've never been happier'.

Then lockdown one ended and there was much rejoicing. I restocked the larder in readiness for lockdown two, which arrived in winter. But something happened: instead of celebrating the solitude and bounty, I became haunted by the inescapable inevitability of dinner. Even now, I gaze at the shelves in the larder in numb despair. I know that something is expected, but I have a cataract of the imagination. My husband worries that our diet of pasta and risotto will give us scurvy. I tell him that the tinned tomatoes and jars of wild-garlic pesto (the fruit of the culinary zeal of lockdown one) will protect us. I remind him we have both received two vaccines, and take vitamin D.

Then there is the memory book of the seasons. The wild garlic that was inspirational in the first lockdown has reappeared in the woods. All I need to do is pick it and I'll recapture the dreamy optimism and energy that inspired all those jars last year. It is harder to fool myself this time, however. The esprit of *Little House on the Prairie* has hit a lull.

To console me, a friend sends me an article from *The New York Times*. It seems that my inability to rise and shine is not unique to me, but is endemic. It's a side effect of the pandemic, and it even has a name: languishing. Which is a relief, because I'd diagnosed late-onset, acute laziness. The word 'languishing' is almost poetry, and makes me think of my Southern grandmothers and great-aunts who worked hard all their lives until they reached a certain age and then entered a more languid period.

Languishing suggests spending mornings in bed with coffee and a good book. Evenings are the smell of gardenias, the second movement of Bach's Brandenburg Concerto No 1 in F Major and a glass of Sauternes. However, that's not, apparently, what languishing now means. It's a new clinical category that slots in as 'not quite depressed', but 'failing to thrive'. Not as serious as a clogged artery, but it renders the languished incapable of concocting a meal from scratch, picking flowers for the table, making an effort cheerfully to oil the wheels of married life.

My husband denies that a diet of snooker, golf and cricket on television is a sign of languishing, despite the fact that he now watches with an intensity I haven't seen before: 'You haven't noticed because we've never been locked up together.' My languishing takes place in the valley of procrastination. I have not cleared the larder, the freezer, the attic or the cellar. I have not written a book or answered urgent letters. I have not dealt with the clutter that surrounds me, although I have read three new books on the subject, books that now add to the clutter. The evening I decided to listen to all six Brandenburgs, I fell asleep.

When I heard the news that Bill and Melinda Gates were calling it quits, it felt like a death in the family. Theirs is a marriage that seemed worthy of a

Nobel Prize for goodness and hope. I also thought, couldn't they have waited until this pandemic is over before cancelling their vows? Waited until Africa was vaccinated and the grief of the past year had faded? Couldn't they quietly languish, for the sake of the world's morale?

Still, learning that the marriage of Mr and Mrs Gates hasn't survived the pandemic made me think we have to adjust those vows: not delete the original ones, but acknowledge that we have to tread softly on the shaky ground of marital quarantine. I will urge my husband not to say 'You've got to give Boris a chance' and to refrain from complaining that 'there's nowhere to sit in the boot room'. I'll advise him never to ask 'What's for dinner?'

For my part, I will endeavour to throw out *The New Yorkers* and copies of the *NY Review of Books* that are years out of date and dominate the bench in the boot room. I'll also wipe away my condescending/quizzical visage that says 'Who did I marry?' when he is watching snooker.

It seems that watching Sky Sports may be an act of defiance against languishing, as much as me reading Nina Stibbe's *Reasons to be Cheerful* when listening to Leonard Cohen. And if the man I married gets scurvy from the pasta diet? I will honour my vow and feed him tea and oranges that come all the way from Waitrose.

May 12, 2021

A LEGACY OF HOPE AND GLORY

Despite my birthplace in the Mississippi Delta and my early years in schools whose teachers tried hard to educate the children in the poorest state in the Union, I reckon I had a head start when I arrived in Suffolk as the bride of a farmer. White children in the Deep South were taught that America owed everything to English literature, English history and English law. As soon as we could recite the Ten Commandments and Psalm 23 by heart, we latched on to Wordsworth, Shelley and Elizabeth Barrett Browning. Our valiant teachers believed it was their bounden duty to civilise us, and the most likely way to achieve that was to Anglicize us. The early emphasis on kings and queens and daffodils meant the native Choctaws and Chickasaws whose land we called our land barely got a mention.

Our history began with Christopher Columbus (two pages and a map of Spain), followed by a whole chapter on Sir Walter Raleigh, adventurer, soldier, poet and favourite of Elizabeth I. In 1584, she granted

Raleigh a royal patent to colonise North America, a dreamy document with a seven-year time limit. The grateful Raleigh named the whole region 'Virginia' in honour of the Virgin Queen, but, unfortunately, the expedition that landed on the island of Roanoke vanished without a trace. For 400 years, the Indians were blamed for this tragedy, but recent theories claim that the English settlers 'happily assimilated' with the natives. The DNA is still out on that, but, in the Deep South, every state has a town called Raleigh.

When my Aunt Libba came to London for my wedding, she made a pilgrimage to Raleigh's tomb near the high altar in St Margaret's, Westminster. She gazed in prayerful silence at the glorious stained-glass window of Raleigh sailing for the Americas, untroubled by the doleful fact that her hero never set foot on the soil of the New World.

The next English expedition to land on a desolate strip of swamp in Virginia in 1607 fared better, but it was an ominous template for the creation of America. These were venture capitalists with get-rich-quick dreams of finding gold. Of the 104 men who sailed forth in three ships, there was one carpenter, two blacksmiths and a flock of footmen. More prophetic still, there were more lawyers than farmers, a perfect recipe for indolence, mutiny and famine on the banks of the James River, a dark marsh that gave them salt poisoning, dysentery and typhoid. Four months after landing, half the men who had sailed on the three ships were dead, including the captain of *Godspeed*, Bartholomew Gosnold.

I didn't know about Gosnold before I came to Suffolk; knew nothing of the village of Grundisburgh where he was born or Otley Hall, his ancestral home, or the market town of Bury St Edmunds, where he lived with his family. In our history books, Gosnold was eclipsed by his friend Capt John Smith, whose life was saved by the beautiful and courageous Pocahontas, daughter of a powerful Indian chief.

It was only after I began life nine miles north of Gosnold's home town that I realised the gap in my American history. In 1602, he sailed from England in a small ship called *Concord*, pioneering a direct route from the Azores to New England and arriving at Cape Elizabeth in Maine. On that trip, he named Cape Cod and discovered a small island he called Martha's Vineyard after his small daughter. Back in England in 1607, he put together a group of investors called the Virginia Company and persuaded James I to grant him a royal patent. Spain had already conquered Mexico and Peru and settled in Florida, the Portuguese were in Brazil, and the French were in Canada. Un-woke as it is to dote on it nowadays, England got a late start to the colonial party.

It would take 100 years and a revolution before America gained its independence from the Mother Country, but, by then, the imprint was fixed. Americans have much to be grateful for, starting with the English language. As Gosnold was looking for investors for his second expedition to America, the Globe Theatre opened with *Macbeth* and the playwright's Sonnets were published.

At the same time, James I was investing in another adventure: 47 scholars in Cambridge, Oxford and Canterbury were assembling to begin their translation of what would be known as the King James Bible. It's not a stretch to say that the language of Shakespeare and the King James Bible that settled on American soil gave dignity to our speech and complexity to our thinking. It would give resonance to the speeches of Churchill, but also to those of Jefferson, Lincoln, Kennedy and Martin Luther King.

With our common language, we crafted our common beliefs: in democracy, in the rights of the individual, in liberty. Our common language has enabled us to share our common goodness, our civilised manners and our morals. Even (take note, Prince Harry) our common laws, including the Bill of Rights.

It hasn't all been plain sailing. Early settlers brought with them guns and slaves, and Americans became overly attached to both. My Virginia-born grandfather shared with H. L. Mencken the belief that civilisation hit its lowest mark where the Anglo-Saxon blood remained undiluted: the Deep South, where the Puritans' gifts of Fundamentalism, Prohibition and Ku Kluxery flourished longest.

I could go on, but this is the moment to dwell on the Best of British. At the top of my 'best' list is a country 3,000 miles away and the precious goal of liberty.

> In the beauty of the lilies
> Christ was born across the sea
> With a glory in his bosom
> That transfigures you and me.
> *Glory, glory, hallelujah.*

June 9, 2021

DRAWING THE LINE

THE Fourth of July came and went without me roaming in the attic for my Stars and Stripes. Considering how long it took me to find a 100% cotton flag with a diminutive 'Made in the USA' label in the seam, you'd think I'd make the effort. For years, the only flags I could find were nylon and 'Made in El Salvador'. And those little flags on sticks children wave in Fourth of July parades? Made in China. I don't believe in 'America First', but I draw the line at American flags made in China.

Actually, I draw the line at a lot of things these days. When I announced (not for the first time) that I was absolutely, resolutely, drawing the line at stuff 'Made in China' in our shop, Sarah, my peerless shop manager, peered over her mask. 'So, no more toys, then?' Paddington Bear, originally made by hand by Jeremy Clarkson's mother, is now made in China. Ditto the sweet Peter Rabbit and Mopsy and Flopsy, the quirky platypus, the endangered pangolin, the wistful teddy bear and my favourite, the velvety hare whose tail you pull and his invisible music box plays

Somewhere Over the Rainbow. Adorable all. And all Made in China.

'We will just expand the Brio toys from Sweden,' I said. You know the ones: the wooden pull-along dachshund, the racing car, the wooden train that parents spend a fortune on and vow to keep forever, an optimistic little heirloom. We inspect the shelves of Brio. The print on the boxes is barely visible: Made in China. I Google 'Brio' on my iPhone. Yep. Made in China since 2004.

It isn't only toys. Last month, I bought a wedding present for a special bride. I've always loved the Georg Jensen 'HK' pitcher, designed by Henning Koppel. Considered 'a landmark of Danish design', it is like a piece of sculpture: slender, elegant, polished stainless steel. When it arrived, I admired it before returning it to its Danish grey box. Then I saw discreet pale letters: 'Designed in Denmark. Made in the P. R. C.' It took a few seconds for the initials to register: People's Republic of China. Georg Jensen! How could you?

I like to think we are a robust citizenry and we could emerge from the Corona Age the way my generation emerged from the hangover years of the 1960s and 1970s. The pot smokers got older, their parents cut them off and they had to get jobs. Before you knew it, they were taking out mortgages, running for political office, playing golf and planting vineyards. People change. The generation that has grown up with Apple everything, IKEA and shipping containers circling

213

the planet loaded down with stuff may draw the line. 'Sustainable' is in the vocabulary now, and 'Made in Britain' has a resonance that P. R. C. lacks.

Not that we will be instantly weaned off the comfort of down jackets from Uniqlo, but it's possible we could all wake up from the Covid-induced slumber and realise that we have been invaded and that the Trojan horse is 'stuff'. It's cheap clothes (and not-so-cheap clothes) and cheap goods (and expensive goods). There is no health in an economy dominated by and dependent on another country.

I'm not saying I'm virtuous, pure or innocent. I'm writing this on an Apple computer (not cheap). It might be 'assembled in Ireland', but it was made in China. Next to my desk is my third iPhone made in China. I bask in the glow of my elegant Anglepoise lamp. British design at its best, it is now made in China. My Hunter wellies were made in Scotland, but that was three decades ago. Now, Hunters are made in China. Despite the spiky Monsieur Macron, I've opted for Aigles, made in France. This morning I checked inside my favourite denim jacket from Seasalt in Cornwall. Made in China. Damn.

I'm married to a man who is a descendant of John Bright, reform politician and defender of free trade. He thinks I'm being neurotic. I point out that our farm account (which is to say, the farm overdraft) is in a bank that is 49% Chinese owned. If that thought drives me to drink, I could take a swig of Abbot Ale from our historic local brewery, Greene King. It is now Chinese-owned. I prefer wine, so the ownership of the brewery in Bury St Edmunds may not affect me as much as the vast nuclear power plant down the road, Sizewell C, that is destined – against fierce resistance – to be built with Chinese investment and French engineering. My husband reminds me that a lot of the investment is from Hong Kong. I call that cold comfort.

With luck, the dystopian sojourn of coronavirus has reminded us how connected this small country is to the whole wide world, that one event (a bat? a virus that escaped from a facility in a country that is powerful and secretive?) can set off a chain of earth-shaking events. It shouldn't have come as a surprise. Farmers are used to witnessing the indivisible harmony of culture and agriculture; the oneness of man, animals, the land, the weather and the family. Touch one and you tamper with them all.

Soon, we will be leaving the predictable shelter of our own walls and returning into the wide world where anything can happen. I'll strive to nurture a modest little utopia Not Made in China. Although this is a double-vaccinated household, I'll tread carefully.

PS: my box of lateral flow tests from the NHS just arrived. Printed in large blue letters on the side of the box: MADE IN CHINA.

Love and hope from your friendly oracle.

July 14, 2021

TERMS OF ENDEARMENT

I NOW check my emails before going upstairs – a vow I made mid-lockdown two: no laptops in bed. Last night, the only email I bothered to read was from my friend Tessa. 'My very, very old cocker spaniel, Betsy, sank her teeth into my hand on Thursday. The pain! It was unprovoked and she gripped me tight, the fleshy part between my thumb and index finger. She is quite blind and deaf, and maybe I startled her. I give her the benefit of the doubt, but we are yet to cuddle again. I am flooded with antibiotics, but my hand is still swollen and bruised and ugly.'

I read the email twice before taking Otis out for his 'finals'. A fox-red labrador whose inner soundtrack is Nina Simone singing 'I wish I knew how it would feel to be free', his late-night routine is to bound off down the farmyard to the gardener's cottage. He then sits outside and barks 'I'm here! I'm here!' until Pip opens the door and gives him a piece of cheese. He has good manners, and never crosses the threshold, but he's as headstrong as a horse in his moonlight bid for freedom and Camembert.

Like Betsy, Otis is now deaf and almost blind. Two years ago, on his routine check-up, the vet had a look at a small sore near his penis. She took a needle biopsy. The diagnosis came a week later: an aggressive tumour. She advised surgery, explaining that it would be 'complicated' because 'it's an area of soft tissue', followed by 'chemo and radiation'. Until that moment I did not know there were veterinary oncologists.

I murmured: 'But he will be 12 years old next month. I'm not sure I should put him through all that.' Worried the young vet might think I was too mean to invest in the medical needs of my dog, I tried to sound casual. 'And the cost? A rough estimate, a ballpark figure?' 'Around £4,000,' she replied. Almost apologetic, I turned down the offer. 'It's not the money,' I said. 'It's his age.'

That was two years ago. Otis now snores softly in his personal sanctuary under my desk. Last year he stopped using the steep back stairs, but comes up the front stairs and arrives in my study before I do. When Merlin, our son and daughter-in-law's six-month-old wire-haired vizsla, comes to visit, Otis is stoic. His cloudy eyes ask 'how long must I endure this?', but he soon forgets his age, plays a bit, nobly shares his toy collection, and practises patience. When Merlin occupies Otis's large bed under the kitchen dresser, Otis curls up in Merlin's bed. I take pictures with my phone. Everyone is happy to let sleeping dogs lie.

All is not well, though. I've always loved the

nonchalant freedom of country dogs who aren't confined to fenced-in yards or kennels. All my dogs have had a routine: checking out the farmyard, investigating the coming and going at the farm workshop, enjoying the woodburners in the cafe in winter, claiming the shade on the restaurant terrace in summer. That freedom ended when Otis began seeing visitors as trespassers. He started barking (frequently, loudly and at nothing visible to the human eye). Then he began growling at visitors, delivery men and customers. Nobody likes a growling dog. Customers are not reassured by 'he's OK, he lives here' or 'he's old and deaf and nearly blind'. They don't believe the owners' dogs have property rights, and they like to say so on Tripadvisor. Now Otis only gets to roam his acres when we're closed.

Other changes have been harder to deal with. Like the dogs in Tottering Hall, Otis enjoys his place at the foot of the bed. I love a dog on the bed, but my husband, unlike Lord Tottering, is quietly long-suffering. A few months ago, Otis and I went to bed early. When my husband came in, my handsome, sweet boy began to snarl like a hound of the Baskervilles. At first we laughed. Then we tried to embarrass him for being so silly. When it happened again, and again, it stopped being funny. Otis now sleeps in the kitchen, and each morning he shows love and joy to the early-rising man who gives him breakfast.

After reading Tessa's email, I sent her an essay

entitled *Hawk* by the American novelist and essayist Joy Williams. Hawk was her beloved German Shepherd. I believe there was never a better dog mother than Miss Williams (and few better writers). One day she took him for a two-day stay at the kennel he knew and liked. When she bent down to give him a goodbye kiss, he suddenly attacked her. It was savage. The bone in her hand was fractured in several places and the tendon torn. The doctor said she had to have surgery immediately: 'The bone could become infected and bone infections are very difficult to clear up.' The expression 'life-threatening' was used.

As soon as I remembered those details I felt like an idiot for sending the essay to Tessa, also a writer. I tried to reassure myself that no bone was broken in Tessa's hand, but then I worried: did she have an X-ray? Am I the kind of alarmist friend no one needs or am I a life saver?

In these bewildering times our dogs have been our salvation. They have given us companionship, devotion, sanity, hope and, we believe, uncritical love. Our happiness has been dependent on them. I hope we haven't harmed them by making their happiness so dependent on us, especially as our terms of endearment are non-negotiable. And maybe we have to accept that dogs share our rage at growing old, and they express it the only way they know how.

August 11, 2021

HOPE AGAINST HOPE

IT'S a cool, grey morning in early September, and the first Christmas cards have arrived. Not cards wishing me a merry Christmas, but a selection via email from *The New York Review of Books* for me to buy. Predictably, the cards are more literary than holy, with drawings by Edward Gorey, Charles Addams and Saint-Exupéry, and they are a welcome distraction on my desktop. I especially like the quote with the man looking out of the window: 'His soul swooned slowly as he heard the snow falling faintly through the universe' (James Joyce).

I was 18 before I saw snow falling through the universe, and I am pretty sure my soul swooned. Soon after that snowfall I came across those words of the Irish writer and took them to heart. That was half a century ago, but this morning I had the feeling that something was missing. I'd like to say that I reached for my volume of *Dubliners* and turned to the last line in the short story 'The Dead'. Instead, I Googled the quote: 'His soul swooned slowly as he heard the snow falling faintly through the universe and faintly falling, like the descent of their last end, upon all the living and the dead.'

The NY Review's abbreviated version is a gently festive message, but the full quote appeals to the poets and the pessimists in the world. Although my commercial verve has hit a lull, I have one more farm diversification up my sleeve: The Melancholy Card Company. I'm always on the lookout for artists with the lugubrious menace of Messrs Gorey and Addams, and I've got a shoebox stuffed with quotes for all dismal occasions. I chose one of my favourites, from Keats's *The Eve of Saint Agnes*, to top the menu in our vineyard restaurant when we re-opened after the first lockdown, 'The hare limped trembling through the frozen grass', but my husband, one of Nature's optimists, vetoed it. 'Too gloomy,' he said, despite the fact that The Leaping Hare was limping, not leaping, which echoed in my poetic ear with 'not waving but drowning'.

If you are inclined to pessimism, these are times that have fertilised every nerve ending. If I hear someone say 'Look on the bright side' or 'You've got to give Brexit a chance', I check to see if the oxygen has been cut off from their brain tissue. When friends tell me that now they have stopped reading newspapers and listening to the news and that they are no longer overeating/spending/drinking and sleep like a baby, I mutter that I think it is healthy to maintain a decent pitch of indignation. The Melancholy Card Company will have a card for these folks: 'A smooth forehead betokens a hard heart' (Bertolt Brecht). That's the thing about us pessimists: we think if you aren't worried sick right now, something's wrong with you.

On days when I feel like Keats's hare, I go in search of my aged copy of Scott Fitzgerald's haunting essay *The Crack-up*. When the writer was overwhelmed with the futility of life, he would try 'resolutely not to think', but to make lists. His lists – of houses he had lived in, popular tunes, suits and shoes he once owned – don't work for me. I find it more helpful to make three lists, not mixing overdue thank-you letters with wildfires.

I start with all the things that weigh me down, but that I can – if only I will – do something about. Then I write down the things that make me sad. My last list is for the things that make me feel crazy with rage. Dealing with the everyday things – clutter, unwritten letters, lost passwords, the expired driving licence, the 10lb I put on in the first lockdown, took off in the second and regained in this grim summer – is not a cure for inertia, but is palliative. It lessens the anxiety that pervades List 2.

The 'Just Sad' list is more complicated, and it seems to grow whenever two or three are gathered together. It's an understanding, a confession, that we have lived and loved in the Best of Times and we didn't know it. We were spendthrift and footloose. We took it for granted that we could travel the world and live wherever we wanted: New York, Paris, London, Kathmandu. We weren't rich, but we had the magical prosperity and dizzy confidence of student grants, cheap rents, jobs we could change like overcoats. *Those were the days my friend, we thought they'd never end.* Now the dice is loaded against our children and against the planet. What were we thinking? (Answer: we weren't thinking.)

It's the third list that causes me to tremble like the hare in the frozen grass. We know the old story of troubles never coming singly, but this is beyond words: Brexit, Covid-19, Hong Kong, China, Russia, floods, wildfires, earthquake in Haiti, Hurricane Ida. The stupefying, mystifying exit from Afghanistan. And a perfect storm of 'not enough': not enough little glass vials for NHS blood tests; not enough lorry drivers, timber or concrete, or midwives, GPs or dentists. Not enough university places or decent houses. Not enough staff for businesses to function or sun for the crops to ripen.

When Fitzgerald finished his lists, he wrote that 'suddenly, surprisingly' he felt better: 'And cracked like an old plate as soon as I heard the news.' When I finish my lists, I feel a more reliable equilibrium. I reckon there is hope for the universe if we don't let ourselves grow accustomed to a planet on fire, a world upside down. Meanwhile, I'm taking orders for the card, *merci à* Rebecca Solnit, that says: 'The tricky thing about hope is not to confuse it with optimism.'

September 8, 2021

THE SUNNY SIDE OF THE STREET

MY last entry had the sombre title 'Hope Against Hope'. Seems some folks were troubled by this. A faithful reader sent an email urging me to 'lighten up'. A friend stopped me in the farmers' market: 'Whoa! I think you need a new playlist!' Her words came back to me this morning as I sat at my desk.

Jessye Norman was singing Richard Strauss's heart-breaking *September*, the haunting words drifting through the room like autumn leaves. Replacing the great soprano with Louis Armstrong is not an easy transition to make, but here goes:

> Grab your coat and grab your hat,
> Leave your worries on the doorstep.
> Just direct your feet
> On the sunny side of the street.

Guess what: Louis's joy had a magical effect. I burst into full voice as I let out the chickens. Some mornings, they look gloomy and suspicious when I open the door to their freedom. This morning, they fluttered around me like tap-dancers in feathers.

My high spirits didn't stop there. Grinding my 100% Arabica/organic/bird-friendly coffee beans felt like a ceremony designed to stave off despair. As the coffee brewed, I counted my blessings: coffee, sourdough toast, blackberry jam and newspapers delivered each morning, safely nestled in the American post box that is identical to the one Snoopy visits to collect his rejection slips for his novels.

Not that I often get to collect the papers. In this household, breakfast is not a shared event. My husband is an early riser, and the early bird gets the papers first. By the time I sit down at the kitchen table, the newspapers in front of me have been filleted, pre-read and christened with traces of marmalade.

I confess that I tend to cast a sceptical eye at those who claim the only way to occupy the sunny side of the street is to cancel the newspapers. I also know that bad news is easier to believe than good news, and the articles that tell you 'Ten Reasons to be Cheerful' always sound simple-minded. It was from this perch – intellectually respectable and morally serious – that I took in the six headlines in the *East Anglian Daily Times*: 'Tankers on their way to Suffolk as government unveils action plan'; 'The 72 postcode areas where Covid infection rates are rising'; '"Poor" infection control at care home sees used Covid test swab left in pile of clean PPE'; 'Invitation-only for booster jabs this autumn and winter'; '400 care workers in Suffolk yet to have single Covid jab, mostly "politically

225

opposed" who are choosing to leave their jobs instead of having mandatory Covid-19 jabs'; 'Suffolk GPs facing increasing abuse from patients'.

Did I read the actual stories? I did not. The headlines sat on the table edge like a roadside bomb, and those four words 'government unveils action plan' threatened to instantly derail my attempt to lighten up. Instead, I refilled my mug, made a second piece of toast, opened *The Times*, and moved boldly on to the prose that always makes life on earth feel more worthwhile: the obituaries.

The hour comes when I have to leave my kitchen sanctuary and face the real world, the one called 'work'. The grape harvest has begun, which is always a time bristling with anxiety and excitement, although this year we have a new and urgent challenge: to find a large van with enough fuel to get the grapes to the winery. This is before we find out that many of our team of pickers are stranded in their rural villages. Meanwhile, the online reservation system of the vineyard restaurant, fully booked throughout October, is now clogged up with cancellations. This might be a blessing, as text messages arrive every few minutes to warn that 'deliveries cannot be guaranteed'. I also have no idea if the man who comes in his tanker each fortnight and fills the large propane gas tank that heats the stoves will be here before the tank is empty.

In this small farming community, we are equally divided between those who blame Brexit for the mayhem and those who blame Covid. Trying to see the sunny side, I trace its roots to the decision of some 400,000 drivers across Europe to return to their homelands during lockdown. Some were furloughed, but many more were simply re-evaluating their lives. This glimpse into a different way of living was not confined to truck drivers. Chefs, builders, roofers, bankers, lawyers, singers, dancers – thousands re-thought the meaning of life.

The lockdown soundtrack was Peggy Lee singing *Is that all there is?*, and, as the world slowly reawakened, workers turned in their passes, bureaucrats returned their laptops, and HGV drivers handed in their keys. The Government elected to run the country was slow to realise that our food and fuel depend on human effort. They know that now, but nobody in the fuel-dependent countryside believes that spreading visas like confetti throughout Poland is going to solve the problem. And who thought visas that will expire on Christmas Eve was a good idea? The sooner they delete Bing Crosby's *I'll be home for Christmas* from the Department for Transport playlist the better.

Although I suspect we will cheer up when things get back to 'normal', I also believe that human happiness grows when people pause and examine their lives. I am convinced that having a job of some kind tends to make folks more cheerful, helps keeps their feet on the sunny side of the street.

Despite the headlines ('Disruption at petrol pumps could last for a month', *The Times*, September 29), I have not succumbed to 'Hope Abandoned'. Like the drivers who decided to stay put in Poland, I, too, have had moments of reflection. Taped to my computer are words from *Flaubert's Parrot* by Julian Barnes: 'It's easy, after all, not to be a writer. Most people aren't writers, and very little harm comes to them.'

October 6, 2021

MILDEW ON THE MAGNOLIAS

I AM shuffling books in my bookstore when a customer comes up to me. Peering over her mask, she says: 'I guess you haven't been back home during all this. Do you ever get homesick?'

It's a friendly question that deserves a friendly answer. I've learned that most folks don't expect a diatribe about the state that believes Donald Trump won the last election. They don't want to hear the heartbreaking news that Mississippi is the first state to reach the morbid milestone of losing one in every 300 residents to coronavirus, and that, if Mississippi were a country, it would have the second-highest per capita death rate in the world, just under Peru. They just wonder if I miss home.

Remembering my manners, I call on Eudora. For more than half a century, Eudora Welty chronicled Mississippi with a truthfulness that was easier for me to latch on to than the intense and entangling chronicles of William Faulkner. Both writers had longish spells out of the South, but both writers came back to their birthplace. Their roaming likely ignited the eternal truths they found in their postage-stamp universe.

It's in this spirit that I turn to Welty, who wrote that: 'A place that ever was lived in is like a fire that never goes out.' I say that I don't miss the heat, that I like picking blackberries in Suffolk because I'm not on the lookout for snakes. I make cornbread in my grandmother's black iron skillet, and grow my own tomatoes. The ones that don't ripen I slice, dip in egg and cornmeal, and fry. I also proudly claim to be bilingual: long ago, I surrendered gas stations and sidewalks, but I talk to my chickens in the pure Southern voices of my great aunts Edna and Blanche.

This wistful journey down Memory Road takes place next to a table that includes books by Flannery O'Connor (Georgia), Ann Patchett (Tennessee) and Faulkner. I point to the slender volume *The Optimist's Daughter*. 'Welty got the Pulitzer Prize for this in 1973,' I say. 'I love it. I read it once a year, and it's like a trip home.'

I'm about to expand on my belief that reading fertilises our memories, and allows us to visit our past without getting hurt, when I see her eyes wander off towards Monty Don over by the gardening table. I can tell that I've given her more than she asked for. I could have told her that talking to strangers is a Southern thing.

As I've got older, I've come to believe that a force more potent than homesickness is the old story of *temps perdu.* It grows as slowly as a tree, and it's in the realm of 'what if?'. Whenever I read Welty, I can't help wondering: 'What if I'd gone back to the South like she did? Would I have buckled down and become a serious writer if I'd stayed put?'

It's not only when I read Welty's work that I feel this way. Last week, a proof copy of Miss Patchett's new collection of essays arrived. I read them all in a day and a night, and then succumbed to an acute case of the 'what ifs', triggered in part by our parallel lives. Miss Patchett lives in her hometown of Nashville, but she went to a small liberal arts college called Sarah Lawrence in New York (so did I). She was the only Southerner there in her day and, 16 years earlier, so was I, although I overlapped with the writer Alice Walker (Georgia) in my first semester. In those days, Southern girls in this New England setting stuck out a mile.

As I read the essays, I kept thinking of all we had in common (did I mention that she also has a bookstore?) and lost track of the differences. For instance, I grew up in the South of civil-rights turmoil; I was in college during the war in Vietnam. Timing powerfully defines our lives. So does biology. She has the precision and discipline of a Swiss watch; I'm easily distracted. I might add that she hates mess, practises Kundalini yoga, is a vegetarian and teetotal. I fall asleep during Pilates class. I raise sheep, and like lamb pink with rosemary and garlic. I planted a vineyard on a south-facing slope on a farm in Suffolk. Even if I'd spent my life surrounded by cotton fields in the Mississippi Delta, I wouldn't have (make that: couldn't have) written *Bel Canto*.

Miss Patchett's new book is called *These Precious Days*, after the final essay she wrote about the first lockdown. The title itself feels prayerful. It also reminded me why I'm not homesick. During lockdown, I made a journey homeward – it just happened to be at the bottom of the farm drive, where I spent my days in a small cottage cataloguing the library of some 400 books on the South and the Civil Rights movement. The collection includes photographs of Mississippi, five taken by Welty in the 1930s, and eight in 1961 by Martin Dain.

In the evenings, I read. I began with the novel I wrote when I was 16, called *Mildew on the Magnolias*, but I only got halfway. Instead, I finally read all the novels by Faulkner I'd never read. Rather like our memories of the places of our past, I'd always liked the idea of Faulkner better than the actual books. Reading him late in life finally cured that.

Those precious days revealed a lot of things. Above my desk is a photograph I found in Oxford, Mississippi, 30 years ago. It was taken in New York in May 1962 when Welty presented Faulkner with the American Academy of Arts and Letters' Gold Medal for Fiction. She tells her fellow Mississippian: 'Mr

Faulkner, I think this medal, being pure of its kind, the real gold, would go to you of its own accord, and know its owner, regardless of whether we were all here to see or not. Safe as a puppy it would climb into your pocket.'

It serves as a poignant reminder that our sense of place is safe as a puppy, and rests in an invisible pocket. Whether we know it or not.

November 3, 2021

VI
Sittin' On The Dock Of The Bay

WONDER AS YOU WANDER

AN email arrived this morning from the Catskills. Every Christmas, my friend David sends me his homemade Pecan Clouds (it's a Southern thing) and alerts me when they're in the post. Today's subject line was worrying: I GIVE UP. He writes that he's finally been defeated by the US and UK postal systems.

I can't say I'm surprised. Last year, his seasonal confection of sugar, egg whites, pecan halves and vanilla extract attracted VAT and duty of £1,000. Although the package weighed less than a hummingbird, was no larger than a bar of Ivory soap, and adorned with a little green sticker stating 'Gift: value $5.00', on its journey to England someone in the postal universe read the value as $5,000.

I was instructed to pay the VAT and duty bill before my package could be delivered. Maurice, the dedicated and much-loved postman in our village, managed to track the origin of the package (Margaretville, NY). I knew at once that it was Pecan Clouds and not a Cartier tank watch sent by an unknown well-wisher.

I declined to fork out the ransom, and the Clouds

made their way back to the land from whence they came. For the record, I try to dissuade anyone from sending a package from the US. If they persist, I plead with them to put 'Gift, No Commercial Value' on the customs slip, even if the package contains emeralds, which they rarely do.

In fact, my friend in the Catskills didn't give up entirely. He surrendered to the great dictator, Amazon. com, and ordered the new collection of poems by a poet I love. As he was about to press SEND, a message appeared: 'Thank you for your order of *Playlist for the Apocalypse* by Rita Dove. Delivery To UK Not Guaranteed.' Those last five words tipped him over the edge of giving, but the poet's title leapt out at me. I immediately ordered it from Blackwell's.

I believe it is prudent to use the word 'apocalypse' sparingly. I also figure the time is right. Lenin said (supposedly): 'There are decades when nothing happens and weeks when decades happen.' The past two years feel as if Lenin was on to something. From the moment a tiny viral particle residing in a bat in China's Hubei Province made its way to the first human, time has moved with the speed of light. Or sound. Whichever is faster. If this doesn't feel apocalyptic, with the new variant multiplying at stupefying speed even as I write this, I don't know what does.

It also happens that I have a playlist for these times. I came late to the playlist thing, but it feels as miraculous as a booster that provides protection in the bipolar world. I no longer linger over BBC Radio 4's *Today*, trembling during over-long dogfight interviews. Instead, I enter the peace of John Williams playing the theme song from *The Deer Hunter*. I kiss my sweet husband and walk my sweet old dog with Arvo Pärt's *Spiegel* on repeat.

My more enlightened friends consider my new routine Meditation for Lightweights, but I no longer grind my teeth as I grind my coffee beans. I don't stomp and swear as I head towards the Guantanamo enclosures where my chickens and turkeys are now confined by law. I think I feel a sense of wonder. My chickens don't know about the bird flu that has robbed them of their freedom – they are simply happy to see me. My Narragansett turkeys don't believe that confinement is their destiny, and they listen intently when I tell them that, although they come from the Suffolk Heritage Turkeys, they are companion birds, not table birds. My vow, tender and uneconomic, is on repeat. I never tire of saying it.

The most eclectic part of my playlist is the 'Christmas Mix' created for me by my friend Susan. Last month, she left her home in Maine, where she has lived for 50 years, and moved to California into a community for 'older adults' in the foothills of the San Gabriel mountains. Her list chimes with this sedentary older adult.

I decorated the tree to Yo-Yo Ma and Alison Krauss's version of *The Wexford Carol*. I set out my crèches to

The Waters of Babylon by Sweet Honey in the Rock and Joan Baez's *I Wonder as I Wander*. Otis Redding sang *White Christmas* as I lit candles, and Whitney Houston joined me over a glass of eggnog, singing *Joy to the World*. By the time King's College Choir sang *How far is it to Bethlehem?*, I felt that comforting sadness of gratitude.

When my book of Rita Dove's poems arrives, I may realise that I'm a lightweight in a troubled world. I'll probably feel guilty that I haven't created a playlist with a moral compass that makes more sense of these times. The truth is, I doubt that even those great Stoics Seneca (about 4BC–AD65) and Marcus Aurelius (AD121–180) could make sense of a pandemic, a planet on fire, NHS waiting lists that have no end, war, famine, pestilence and cruelty to children in our midst. The best we can do is try to find ways to cope when life seems beyond our control.

Meanwhile, I'm trying to figure out how to put Charlie Brown on my playlist. He's my kind of Everyman Stoic, and he tells Lucy how to face life's adversities and live well in the world: 'Be kind. Don't smoke. Be prompt. Smile a lot. Eat sensibly. Avoid cavities and mark your ballot carefully. Avoid too much sun. Send overseas packages early. Love all creatures above and below. Insure your belongings and try to keep the ball low.' I would add: put Judy Garland singing *Have Yourself a Merry Little Christmas* on repeat. Always and forever.

January 5, 2022

THE MISSISSIPPI TRUTH

YOU'D think I might be embarrassed to write about truthfulness. And, if not embarrassed, I'd at least feel a little shameful. The truth is, where I come from, the clean-as-a-bone truth is never appreciated as much as a good story that provides an extra crackle to the beat of life. Southerners can lie with the sincerity of angels. Here on this ancient patch of land in Suffolk where the fields are as flat as the Delta, it's called The Mississippi Truth.

I could wander further down this road and tell you the reason that there are so many Southern writers is because we love telling stories (regrettably now called 'the oral tradition'). There are a lot of theories about this: it's because we lost the war; because we are born with a sense of 'place'; because we never replaced our King James Version of the Bible. All these theories feel shop worn nowadays, and I side with the writer Roy Blount Jr on this. Born and raised in Georgia, Roy blames the heat. He reckons that it gets so hot in the South you can't breathe, and writing is a job you can do in the shade. He also believes that writing is a way of resting from our favourite oral traditions: eatin' and drinkin' and talkin'.

You can probably guess where I'm going with this. Yep: much as we love a good story, there's a heap of difference between a good story and a bad lie. As William Faulkner or John Grisham might put it, telling good old stories on the screen porch is not the same as wilful, vicious, pernicious, crafty, self-serving, pusillanimous, bizarre and horrendous lying.

I grew up with good old stories and bad lies, and I honestly can't remember when I could tell the difference. I'd like to say it was when I noticed that the white schools had grass lawns, boxwood hedges and shiny yellow school buses, and the black schools were surrounded by patches of mud and dirt and hand-me-down buses that were no longer considered good enough for the backsides of white children. Did I suddenly know in my heart that 'Separate but Equal' was a lie? Probably not. When you live in the Land of Lies, you tend to miss the obvious.

Somewhere along life's highway, I began to find the lies told by politicians and their enablers was like drinking punch made with Southern Comfort: a glass goes down easily enough, but two helpings and you end up sick as a dog. It hurts to think of all the big lies I've witnessed: the revelations of the Pentagon Papers about the lies told about the war in Vietnam;

the fetid swamp of Watergate lies; Saddam's 'Weapons of Mass Destruction', now classified as a 'failure of intelligence'. That lie ripped the world apart in our lifetime and for the lifetime of our children's children. Proof – in case we needed it – that a single lie can undo a lifetime of peace.

It's humiliating for politicians to be accused of lying, but it's the word-shuffling denials that are degrading. Remember how, when he was first running for President, Bill Clinton was asked if he'd ever used drugs? He admitted he'd tried marijuana when a student at Oxford. He should have stopped right there, yet he went on to say he smoked but he 'didn't inhale'. Perhaps that reflective use of language should have prepared us for his response when asked if he'd had sex in the White House with a 22-year-old intern: 'I want to say one thing to the American people. I want you to listen to me... I did not have sexual relations with that woman. Miss Lewinsky.'

This linguistic tap dance was worthy of Fred Astaire: 'sexual relations' – shuffle-shuffle-wing-step – are not the same as 'sexual encounters' – shuffle-shuffle-ball change. Looking mournful and ashamed, he admitted that what he'd done was wrong, inappropriate and blameworthy, and he truly felt real bad about it. But, he insisted, then and evermore, that he did not lie. At least, not according to the dictionary definition of 'sexual relations'. He survived his impeachment, and if you were a

Democrat you thought Kenneth Starr was a whole lot nastier than the President – who always was a hard dog to keep under the porch.

Since time began, I reckon folks have been pretty tolerant of scamps. Mostly, they preferred ignorance. My grandmother was glad FDR had a 'loving companion' because she thought Eleanor Roosevelt wasn't wifely. I'm glad I didn't know about JFK's scampering until years afterward, and, even now, I wish I could unknow it. Actually, I have a long list of 'what I wish I didn't know', because what I hold fast to now, what I yearn for, is thoughtfulness, intelligence, depth, truthfulness. I might add: kindness, an ability to use words, gracefulness – and probably good hair and teeth. A mix of Jimmy Stewart, Jimmy Carter and Tom Hanks.

I'm not naming names, but here's what I'm sick and tired of: anarchy, serial dishonesty, sloth, high drama, bar-room brawls even when they are called work, dogma and off-the-hoof populism. I've lived long enough to know that life's not worth living if we don't hold fast to truth. Truth is a rock. Chip away at it enough and you end up with gravel, then sand.

I'm Southern-born, and I write about my late-in-life conversion to the hard truth with some nervousness. It is hard to relinquish the creed bestowed at birth, 'never let the truth interfere with a good story', and even now I can't resist ending with a good story. It sure sounds true to me. When Barbara Bush was asked what she thought about Clinton's nimble approach to language, she didn't even bat an eye. 'Clinton lied. A man might forget where he parks his car or where he lives, but he never forgets oral sex, no matter how bad it is.'

Long live truth and the oral tradition – eatin', drinkin' and talkin'.

February 2, 2022

THE ENDURING SEARCH FOR
ENDURANCE

I AM sitting at my desk in a Suffolk manor house that
is a collage of dates: 1585, 1640, 1920. My study was
once the housekeeper's bedroom. Today, Wyken has
no live-in housekeeper, and the occupant who writes
this was not to the manor born.

All the places we've ever lived have a way of
imprinting our lives. I was born on the banks of the
Yazoo – Choctaw for River of Death. It's a good
name for a muddy tributary of the Mississippi that
is deadly when it floods, deathly when the flat land
surrounding it reaches 100°C at dawn. My legacy
from this land of heat, cotton and copperheads? A
lifelong yearning for... snow. A love of the world
of white-on-white that I knew only through
photographs, movies and books.

Another place that enriched my nomadic life was
Putney Heath. The friend who introduced me to the
man who installed me in this manor house coached
me, 'Don't go on about how much you love Putney.
It sounds so suburban' – but I loved the flat carved

out of the first floor of an Edwardian house. Five days after I moved in, the blizzard of December 1981 transformed my new universe. It was a sign. Before the snow had melted, I learned that, from 1911 to 1913, Ernest Shackleton, his wife Emily and their three children had lived in my house.

Not that I knew a lot about the heroic polar explorer when I arrived at No 7, Heathview Gardens. I knew North was the Arctic (polar bears) and South was Antarctica (penguins, no polar bears). In Mississippi, a land half in love with defeat, it was Robert Falcon Scott who was revered. English, courageous, a lover of Russian novels and the poetry of Tennyson, he was the tragic hero who, in 1912, reached the South Pole 34 days after Amundsen planted the Norwegian flag in the snow. Two months later, Scott and what was left of his gallant team pitched their second-rate tent, tucked themselves into their reindeer-hide sleeping bags, and entered the sleep that polar explorers know will be their last. The most heartbreaking part of the story: they were only 11 miles from One Ton Depot, with its plentiful supplies.

The other arctic explorer we learned about was the American Admiral Richard Byrd. The first person to fly over the North Pole and, later, the South Pole, it was the five months he spent alone in an underground shack in Antarctica in 1934 that fascinated me. One summer, I found a copy of *Alone*, his account of that journey. He believed he would spend his time reading and listening to classical music on his wind-up record player, but, a month in, he realised the fumes from his oil-burning stove were poisoning him. 'What I had not counted on was discovering how close a man could come to dying and still not die, or want to die,' Byrd wrote. Read enough memoirs of polar exploration, including Ranulph Fiennes, and you realise it is a sombre theme.

Shackleton and his epic journey across the treacherous Weddell Sea soon became my obsession. He is also at the centre of the modest, if unlikely, polar shrine in this manor house. I have 40 books on polar exploration, including maps and journals. Thanks to the archives of the Royal Geographical Society, I have 10 photographs by Frank Hurley, the official photographer of the Endurance expedition. I live with his legendary images: *Endurance* strangled by ice, the men pulling the open boats over land, and the dogs, the dogs who trusted the men who led them into this white danger (that story is too sad to tell here).

Every evening, I log on to follow another expedition. A century after *Endurance* was crushed by ice and sank, a state-of-the-art South African icebreaker, *Agulhas II*, with a crew of 46 and a team of scientists, has gone in search of her. Financed by an anonymous donor at a cost of more than $10 million, the expedition, Endurance22, has only two weeks and two underwater drones to locate and survey the lost ship, which is sitting in 10,000ft of water in what

Shackleton described as the 'worst sea in the world'.

I follow Endurance22 in various podcasts. Tonight, the icebreaker is stranded in pack ice just like *Endurance*, a reminder that ice is a brutal dictator that doesn't respect tenacity, courage, modern technology and science. The marine archaeologists think they are close to the right spot – give or take a few miles – based on the calculations of the ship's captain, Frank Worsley, whom *Endurance* obsessives believe was the real hero of the greatest survivalstory in exploration.

The $10 million cost of the expedition also stayed in my mind. Alongside my nightly tracking of Endurance22, I began searching for a photograph of the Putney house when Shackleton lived there. I found mention of it – Shackleton, always on the edge financially, worried the house added to his woes – but no family photograph. Instead, I discovered that the house is for sale. Turned back into a single dwelling, it now sits behind two imposing gates and a high fence. It has the whiff of oligarchy about it, with a swimming pool and a pool house in the garden where I once planted roses from Peter Beales and tree peonies that were beyond my means. The price tag is almost exactly the cost of the Endurance22 expedition in the Weddell Sea.

One thing gives me peace of mind. If *Endurance* is found, drones will take photographs and make laser scans of the wreckage, but the site won't be disturbed. It was declared a historic monument under the terms of the Antarctic Treaty signed in 1959 'to preserve the continent for peaceful purposes'.

I wish I could say the same for my – and Shackleton's – old house. You might think its significance is emotional, not historical, but I believe one of those round blue plaques would have been a more valuable addition than a swimming pool.

March 2, 2022

The expedition to find the *Endurance* was successful. It was located about four miles south of where Capt. Frank Worsley had noted the ship's location back in 1915. The name ENDURANCE was still visible on her stern.

TIME AND AGAIN

DURING the first lockdown, I made more vows than a virginal novice in her noviciate. I vowed to learn at least one *Goldberg Variation* on the ancient Bechstein that presides in lonely silence in the drawing room. I vowed to memorise a sonnet or two, and to pick, make and fill the freezer with wild-garlic pesto. I'd write long-overdue letters and clear the linen cupboard of three generations of long, white tablecloths. I promised to edit book shelves.

Well, I made the pesto. If I'm not wracked with guilt, it is because I believe that remorse rarely produces renewal and reform. Those memories returned this week as I filled my French grape-picking basket with wild garlic and remembered that those pots of pesto provided intense flavour to the grey second lockdown. I felt a similar spark of relief this morning when I went to the shelf where three decades of my monthly 'at-a-glance' diaries reside. In my lockdown piety, I'd consigned them to the recycle bin, then had second thoughts and fished them out. I retrieved the year 2014 with ease.

When I say 'diaries', I don't mean the kind of journals written by Virginia Woolf and Frances Partridge. Mine are spiral notebooks that allow me to keep track of where I'm supposed to be, appointments that most people now keep on their phones. Inky words tracking the days and months of 2014 are a record of trade fairs in January, staff meetings, tasting sessions at the winery, pruning in the vineyard, tickets for *Eugene Onegin*, appointments in St James's with Mr Badger to unravel my US taxes, and, in large letters, 'CARDIAC ARREST', a shock reminder of the February day my husband ordered a breakfast of scrambled eggs and bacon in his London club before silently sinking to the carpeted floor.

A kitchen porter witnessed the fall, a member of staff grabbed the defibrillator that had never been used, an ambulance arrived in six minutes, and for the next five days the doctors in ICU at St Thomas's warned me in soft voices to 'prepare for the worst'. According to the diary, however, 10 days later he was back home, fitted with an ICD (implantable defibrillator), and driving around the fields in his ancient pick-up truck looking for grey partridges.

It's a good thing to keep track of miraculous events in your life, although that wasn't my intention as I searched through my only written record of 2014. In fact, I was looking for something else: the Russian invasion of Ukraine. I found nothing. On the farm, we keep records of rainfall and crop yields, but world events tend to go unrecorded. I noted precisely when the ram was introduced to the ewes, but the small and not insignificant European war isn't mentioned.

You may wonder why I'm looking for it now. Because, like half the people I talk to each week in the farmers' market, I start the day with the *Today* programme, end with the BBC news, wake up in the middle of the night and turn on the World Service. I am living in the shadow of a war that looms large in all our lives. I now know that Ukraine is the size of Spain. I can locate Crimea, occupied and claimed by Russia in 2014, Donetsk and Lugansk, 'self-proclaimed People's Republics in 2014', on the map that is as familiar as our chefs' tattoos. I can point to Odesa and, late in the day, I know where a once-beautiful city called Mariupol is located. Most evenings, I look closely at the map with red arrows that show where the refugees are fleeing: Poland, Romania, Moldova. I've become attached to the voices above the maps, standing in the war-torn streets. The reporters, like the Ukrainian soldiers, are heroes of our time.

Life in the countryside can feel like a retreat from the worst that can happen, a world where the hedgerows define the fields and narrow our lives. It happens naturally.

This morning we sold 58 tons of wheat at £303 a ton. Back in November we sold 'forward' at £150 a ton. We're not in a festive mood, however. We're wide-eyed at the price of fuel that runs the tractors that pull the harrow. We're trying out alternatives to fertiliser that's doubled in price – planting white clover under the wheat to lock in the nitrogen – hoping to increase the yields that produce the crops that feed the world. No farmers I know are celebrating because, in Ukraine, 'the bread basket of the world', farmers can't drill their fields. The vast arable plains of Suffolk and Norfolk have no fences to protect us from the reach of war.

Something else survived my 'cleansing' vow, and still languishes on a desktop. It's a little block of concrete the size of a stocking stuffer, sent to me by my nephew who was stationed in Germany when the Berlin Wall came down. The little hunk of the wall now feels like a *memento mori* that belongs in the book of lost words, words such as *glasnost*. Call it 'concrete for thought', and remember it when we are told that Putin wants a divided Ukraine 'like Korea'. Or, closer to home, like the tragedy of East Germany and West Germany.

It won't surprise you that a man who survives a cardiac arrest is one of Nature's optimists. He looks at President Zelensky and sees a wise and passionate leader who is a powerful force for historic change. The farmer's wife looks at the blue-and-yellow bunting hanging in the farmers' market and wonders how many landmines will be removed with the £1,200 we've raised for the HALO Trust in Ukraine.

Ukrainian *borscht* is now on the menu in the restaurant, with all proceeds going to the Polish Humanitarian Action fund. People are generous, but I wonder for how long? This will be a long war. Unlike the invasion in 2014, which never appeared in my diary, there is now a sense that the future of Ukraine and the future of Europe's east and west depends on what happens. This feels like Europe's cardiac arrest. Hope against hope.

April 6, 2022

A COUNTRYWOMAN'S NOTES

THIS morning, two letters arrived in the post. The writer in the first is offering me a 'personal treasure': a collection of *Country Life* that dates back to 1980. I have to admit this is not the first such offer that's come my way. Over the years, I've been offered collections that go back to before The Queen was The Queen, when historic architecture was black and white, articles were twice as long, and Frontispiece girls were Christian virgins in pearls on the eve of matrimony.

The writers are always polite. They inquire if I would like to purchase their collection or, failing that, advise them of potential buyers. One asked if I knew any likely Anglophiles in America. The more modest hope I might know of a good home for their copies, requesting only that they collect in person.

I am charmed by these letters, but, the truth is, I have my own magazine mountain to deal with. Mine is not archived by date, but is a haphazard mix of three decades piled on the steps of the back stairs. Like the canary in the coal mine, Otis, my old labrador, long ago sensed the danger and hasn't risked this route of ascent since 2014. Avalanches of *Country Life* are not unknown in this house, but I have made one concession to health and safety: the threatening stacks aren't on the bannister side.

Inspired by today's correspondent, however, I Googled 'Back copies of *Country Life*' to explore the market. In an instant, the second-hand-book site www.abebooks.co.uk appeared with a single offer from a rare-book dealer in Bath: a collection of 11 volumes (Vol. XCIX) 1946, January to June, to (Vol CXV) 1954. Grandly described as '...uniformly bound in quarter morocco binding, signed Sangorski and Sutcliffe', the magazine itself has to settle for the rather more prosaic 'primarily concerned with rural communities and their environment although much of its success was built on its coverage of country houses, architecture, and gardening, including reviews of books, wine, art and architecture'. The seller's elaborate account of the collections' provenance would excite Julian Fellowes.

The row of ivory-white leather volumes looks substantial and elegant in the photographs, although only one volume is open. It reveals the Frontispiece of January 18, 1946: 'Lady Irene Astor is the youngest daughter of the late Field Marshal Earl Haig and the late Countess Haig and was married last October to Captain Gavin Astor, the Life Guards, eldest son of Colonel the Hon J. J. and Lady Violet Astor.'

257

I read the words in a trance. Things being what they are in the world, I look at most things in a trance these days, but the subdued portrait of Lady Irene brought me back to reality. I saw a newly wed woman whose parents did not live to see her marry. A long world war has just ended. She marries a soldier of that war. It is a moment in history recorded in *Country Life*. It's not the 'paper of record'. It's a more poignant record.

The second letter is also from a reader who is parting with stuff. She writes that she is 'transitioning(!) from Georgian house to bungalow in my daughter's garden'. She adds that 'while ditching the clutter I found your column from September 2011, the 10th anniversary of 9/11, about the composer Arvo Pärt and his... Spiegel im Spiegel. See enclosed'.

I had forgotten that column. I remember the music – I like the version played by Tasmin Little – but I forgot that Mr Pärt was born in Estonia on September 11, 1935, and that, five years later, Estonia was occupied by the Soviet Union. I forgot that the composer's early works were banned by the Soviet censors, and he went through long periods of contemplative silence, years when he didn't write a single note. I even forgot that when the Russian journalist Anna Politkovskaya was murdered in 2006, the composer dedicated all his works performed in the following year to her, declaring that she 'staked her entire talent, energy and – in the end – her life on saving the victims of the abuses prevailing in Russia'.

I also forgot Auden's prophetic poem *September 1, 1939*, where he writes 'Our civilisation is ever fragile... our world in stupor lies'. Forgot the words of the evolutionary biologist Stephen Jay Gould, whose life's work had led him to believe 'in the overwhelming predominance of simple decency and goodness, a central aspect of our being as a species, yet so easily obscured by the rare act of spectacularly destructive evil'; his belief in 'tough hope and steadfast human nature'.

How did I forget all this? How did the world forget?

The morning's letters reminded me that, in this fast-moving transitory world, *Country Life* is a rare thing: a magazine with roots that go deep into the land. It has an unwritten motto: Slow down. Look up. Look at beauty. Make room for Nature. Honour the otters and the red squirrels (Ian Niall's '*A Countryman's Notes*'). Don't take lilies for granted (Christopher Lloyd). Fix the mess we've made of the planet, field by field, river by river.

Country Life has the heft and usefulness of a Sussex trug, the simple majesty of a medieval tapestry, the gaiety of Noël Coward, P. G. Wodehouse and *The Vicar of Dibley*. It is a record of the times we live in, a predictor of the future, and a useful reminder that even in uncertain times we have to hold on to what delights and sustains us.

PS: The asking price of the 11 leatherbound volumes of *Country Life* (1946–54) is £4,500. During those seven years, farmland was selling for £80 an acre. Not everything you read here is a blueprint for peace of mind, but, hey – nothing lasts 125 years without tough hope.

May 11, 2022

HAPPY AND GLORIOUS

I CAN'T remember when I last used my 12 Fabergé after-dinner coffee cups. Americans call these little cups '*demi-tasse*', which is about as bilingual as we get. Mine come in five colours, and I treasure them, although I've reached the age where my guests are fewer in number and tend to opt for mint tisanes after dinner.

I first saw Fabergé porcelain at Mount Congreve in Ireland, where Ambrose Congreve adhered to the *ancien régime* of separating after dinner. The men adjourned to the 'smoking room' to enjoy Cuban cigars and Port, and the women were guided to the 'little drawing room' for coffee. When I admired the exquisite little cups, Geraldine, the chatelaine, grinned as she revealed their provenance: copies of the Royal Collection from the Buckingham Palace Shop. I could hardly wait to acquire my own.

Over the years, I've been a loyal subject of the realm in that shop. I bought copies of The Queen's brooches for my great aunts in Mississippi, and God

Save The Queen tea towels by the dozen. I've filled my suitcase with royal biscuit tins tucked inside royal tea cosies on trips back home. My sister begins her visits to England at The Queen's Gallery shop.

On the occasion of The Queen's 90th birthday, we went to the exhibition in the Palace, 'Fashioning a Reign: 90 Years of Style from The Queen's Wardrobe'. We stared at the jodhpurs of the 10-year-old Princess. In the space of that year – 1936 – there were three reigning monarchs: George V, her grandfather, who died on January 20; Edward VIII, who abdicated on December 11; and his successor, George VI. The jodhpurs look so small. Only afterwards did we realise that they were worn by a little girl whose destiny changed before she outgrew them. We were too dazzled by the immaculately tailored suits and the sumptuous wasp-waist evening gowns of the glamorous Queen. If we'd found a Hartnell or Amies copy in the palace shop, we'd probably have put it on Visa in a heartbeat.

All this royal acquisitiveness has given rise to the belief in my American family that I am on friendly terms with The Queen. It seems heartless to disappoint. True, I've attended two garden parties where I've seen The Queen in the distance, but the best detail I can offer is the recipe for the very good iced coffee, revealed by a discreet member of staff. The secret ingredient: a dash of Camp coffee.

There is one sentence I can honestly begin with the

words 'The Queen and I'. It happened at the Chelsea Flower Show the year they decided to dispense with the sit-down 'tea' for the Royal Party and have a stand-up 'cocktail'-style gathering instead. I was talking to Joanna Bennett, wife of the show director, when I suddenly saw the two men who'd been speaking to The Queen walk away. The Queen was suddenly left on her own.

'Good heavens!' I whispered to Joanna, 'The Queen has been abandoned.' Off we went. After an awkward curtsey, the only morsel of conversation I could come up with was 'I'm a close neighbour in Suffolk of the Duchess of Grafton'. The Duchess, with the perfect name of Fortune, was The Queen's Mistress of the Robes, the senior lady in the Royal Household (and, no, she does not look after The Queen's clothes and jewellery – she is the friend and confidante who accompanies The Queen at state ceremonies and on royal tours).

'Oh dear. Poor Fortune. The Duke is so unwell,' The Queen replied. Actually, she said rather more, but I believe you aren't supposed to reveal these conversations, although for years I dined out on 'The Day I Rescued The Queen'.

When my American friends ask me to verify incidents that take place in *The Crown*, they are shocked to learn that I don't watch it. I did start – I loved Claire Foy and I loved the clothes – but Matt Smith's Prince Philip made me squirm, and I staunchly deny events of which I am completely ignorant. I realise that it's late in the day to object to *The Crown* because it makes the monarchy into a soap opera. That began with the invention of the printing press.

It's also time to let go of Walter Bagehot's proverbial belief that the monarchy's 'mystery is its life. We must not let in daylight upon magic.' The Queen he was writing about was Victoria, and the era was free of radio, television, social media, cameras with long lenses and on-screen confessionals with Bashir, Dimbleby and Oprah.

Still relevant, however, is Bagehot's definition of the powers of the monarch, 'the right to be consulted, the right to encourage, the right to warn'. These powers aren't magic. They call for stamina, devotion, intelligence and almost inhuman discipline, qualities The Queen has displayed in abundance. Think of all those boxes. All those Prime Ministers. All those state visits and ceremonies. All the jubilees! More than any ancient building or marble statue, she represents her kingdom's history and continuity. She makes the country she reigns over feel good about itself, even in times when few things encourage that feeling.

As much as they admire and adore The Queen, what I am asked most by Americans is: why doesn't she retire, enjoy her twilight years, abdicate in favour of her long-attendant son? When the former American ambassador Raymond Seitz asked that question of the canon showing him around Westminster Abbey, the reply was solemn and swift: 'Oh no,' he said. 'You see, she's been anointed.' That's a realm of spirituality that is perplexing for most Americans.

Meanwhile, we are celebrating the jubilee here at Wyken. I've made coronation chicken, but, instead of the winning trifle, I've made The Queen's own favourite dessert – lemon posset, served in my Royal Collection Fabergé *demi-tasse*.

I've also hung the vintage bunting from the Golden Jubilee that spells out the royal motto '*Dieu et Mon Droit*'. I'm pretty sure it does not mean 'God is my finger'.

June 1, 2022

ALL THE PRESIDENT'S MEN

MY new job is dog-sitting for my grand-dog, Merlin, a 14-month-old wire-haired vizsla who has the bone structure of a kangaroo. His parents can't WFH, so Merlin spends his days with us. The resident Old Dog practises labradorial transcendental meditation in the presence of the charismatic Young Dog.

Providing day care for Merlin has activated feelings long overdue. When I moved to Paris in my twenties, I deposited most of my worldly goods in my parents' basement, including all my chattels with US voltage – typewriter, stereo, coffee grinder – and boxes of photographs, old letters, diplomas, books, worn copies of the anti-war newspaper I'd edited. I also left my dog.

The decision to leave the country was impetuous. I didn't speak French, I didn't have a trust fund, and, despite a university degree, I lacked any 'vital skills'. Abandoning my two-year-old Weimaraner was irresponsible. I look back on my parents' willingness to adopt their grand-dog with late-in-life gratitude. They were bewildered, but tolerant when I announced my decision to move to Paris when Nixon resigned. The new chapter in the history of the country felt like a good time to start a new chapter in my life.

My parents became devoted to my dog, but they were less attached to my stuff. Every trip home, my mother would urge me to edit the boxes. Over the years, I gave my typewriter and stereo to nephews, consigned the newspapers to recycling, and ditched letters of doubtful historical interest. During one exorcism of stuff, I pulled out a stiff grey objet d'art 12in by 18in and put it in the bottom of my suitcase. Two decades later, I got it framed. A couple of weeks ago, I hung it on the wall above my desk.

From a distance, it looks like Minimalist art in a shade that Farrow & Ball might call Lonesome Dove. Close up, you can make out the letters. At the top, in Old Gothic font: *The Washington Post*. Below, in bold 2in-tall letters: **Nixon Resigns**.

The technical word for my relic is 'flong', the relief impression created from the handset metal type that, for 300 years, was how newspapers were printed. I didn't know the legendary team of Watergate reporters, Bob Woodward and Carl Bernstein – I was a lowly 'stringer' – but from my school days hanging out at the local town paper I'd loved the sounds and smells of the print room, admired the speed and skill of printers. When Nixon resigned on August 9, 1974, one of the *Post*'s printers presented me with the historical flong because it was my birthday. I saved it for 50 years because it felt like a piece of history: Nixon's and mine.

If I thought the French would be aglow with admiration for the legendary Watergate reporters, I was wrong. The French thought Nixon's resignation preposterous and petty, the saga of Watergate proof that Americans are puritanical and politically naïve.

The English had a different concept of justice, and they had the advantage of Alistair Cooke's *Letter from America*. His broadcasts on Watergate are unmatched. With perfect pitch, clarity and detail, he records history as it unfolds. From his letter of September 17, 1972, he began his account of June 17, when five men with cameras and bugging equipment were caught burgling the offices of the Democratic National Committee in the building complex known as the Watergate. The leader of the bungled raid was a former employee of the CIA. Cooke may have been slow to pick up on the story, but he stayed with the elephantine unfolding over the next two years, making dozens of broadcasts. He didn't stop with the one and only resignation of an American president. Twenty years later, he covered the funeral of Nixon. Last week, roaming around iPlayer, I found Cooke's broadcast on the 25th anniversary of Watergate. I listened in amazement.

I probably sound like a 'Watergate junkie', obsessed with every detail of the biggest political scandal of the 20th century. I'm not. I'm bemused the word has become the moniker for every scandal – 'partygate', 'beergate' – but I haven't wallowed in Watergate. Last week, however, I froze when I heard a familiar American voice on Radio 4's *Today*. It was the anniversary of the event, and the interviewee was drawing a line from the Watergate break-in of 1972 to the insurrection at the US Capitol in 2021. It was John Dean, who had been recruited from the Justice Department to the Nixon White House as a legal counsel. Mr Dean was 31 years old when he publicly turned against Nixon by testifying to the Senate Watergate committee, accusing the President of being directly involved in the cover-up. Fifty years later, I listened to him saying he has never been more concerned about US democracy than he is now because 'the country is more polarised today than it was during Watergate and Fox News feeds that polarisation'.

Most evenings, my husband and I watch the January 6 hearings on CNN. It feels like a reincarnation of my parents watching the Watergate hearings. I can almost hear the tinkle of ice in their bourbon and water. Each night I say 'Trump's behaviour eclipses Nixon's'. Each night, my husband replies 'The root of their sins is the same: to undermine elections in a democracy'.

For days I've lamented that there is no Mr Dean, no one of conscience with the courage to speak the truth. Then it came: the 25-year-old former aide to

Mr Trump's Chief of Staff. Cassidy Hutchinson's testimony was as powerful and shocking as Mr Dean's 50 years earlier. Her testimony might not change history, but, with her calm, precise and courageous testimony, history rhymed.

Another thing Mr Dean said on *Today*. 'Nixon had a conscience. He experienced shame. I doubt if Trump does.' We never really know who is capable of shame, but when any man – or woman – is determined to stay in power whatever the electorate says, democracy may be given up for lost. It's a truth worth hanging on the wall.

July 6, 2022

THE FIRE THIS TIME

THE week before the temperature in Suffolk reached 39°C, we were sitting in the garden on a cool, moonshiny evening. It was pure joy because we were drinking our sparkling Wyken Moonshine with our friends James and Kerry, toasting 'Friends Reunited'. Last month, they moved back to England after living in Napa Valley in California for nearly 30 years.

Against a backdrop of gentle breezes, we listened to the story of how they left a world of miraculous beauty, stupefying wines and a rural homestead with, as far as the eye could see, vineyards – a patch of paradise on earth. The kind of dreamy landscape that I've been trying to create on this Suffolk farm for the 33 years we've known each other.

In soft voices, they told about their journey. It began with a fire or, rather, an evacuation – actually, three evacuations in three years as the wildfires came ever closer. They described living with the emergency bag always by the front door. This isn't a piece of carry-on luggage: it's the bag you grab as you flee: water and food, mobile-phone charger, flashlight, masks to filter the toxic air, medications, first-aid kits, cash, vital documents.

After the first evacuation, Kerry organised four decades of photographs. She shipped the albums, together with precious records of their lives, to their daughters in London: 'I needed to save the story of their childhood.'

Even before the second evacuation, they had begun to redesign their lives in that once-upon-a-time idyllic part of the world. 'We went overboard with every safety measure. We pulled out the garden around the house and replaced it with gravel. We put on a fire-retardant roof with an automatic sprinkler system that we could operate remotely. That was a miracle. Most houses, even vineyards, which can be firebreaks, are now denied insurance for fire.'

Then came the third evacuation. This time, the flames burned within 400ft of their front door. 'Our property survived, but devastation was all around us with the sure threat of more to come. We knew we needed to sell up, to move 6,000 miles back to the UK.

'We are climate refugees, but we are the very lucky. Our daughters live and work here. James's three sisters are here and the world of cousins and family is large and welcoming.' Six months were spent getting ready to sell the property. Furniture and belongings were dispersed to friends and charities, as a lifetime's possessions were edited down to the 'loved and irreplaceable' and fitted into a 7ft by 7ft container, the size of the crates that transport grapes from vineyard to winery during harvest.

Those treasures are now in the two-bedroom London flat a 10-minute walk from each of their daughters and their one-year-old granddaughter. They resist words such as 'resilient', but admit to a persistent sense of relief, the wordless happiness that comes when the fear of wind-whipped flames no longer governs your days.

Over the weekend, I looked guiltily at my over-filled rooms. This is a house that accumulates stuff. For years, I've been tormented by something Wendell Berry wrote in his *Farming: a Hand Book*, 'Don't own so much clutter that you will be relieved to see your house catch fire'. This is not the time to dwell on that. Instead, I make piles of old curtains, soup bowls, books, stacks of *New Yorkers* – anything I can persuade James and Kerry to take with them.

In the days after their visit, I became obsessed with the terror they experienced as the fires came ever closer, of living with the smoke that blew across the miles from Lake Tahoe, from the deadly fire in a town called Paradise. Mercifully, it seemed far away. And then it wasn't. Suddenly, the whole world was on fire. On the hottest days in this country's long history, we watched the news as massive wildfires spread through France, Italy, Spain, Greece, Portugal, Australia, Yosemite. It was like watching *Apocalypse Now* on a loop, without the Hueys and the *Ride of the Valkyries* soundtrack, only the skeletons of houses, cars, swing sets and trampolines: the material evidence of ordinary lives, of human cost beyond measure.

If there was comfort in knowing that what we were witnessing was far from this island kingdom, suddenly we saw Wennington, a village of 300 people, in Essex, the county next door to Suffolk – 19 houses destroyed. I watched the news again and again, trying to understand the scope and randomness of the destruction: a row of houses gone, edged on each side by others that survived, a lone church of stone still standing. Then I saw a bare patch, a field beyond the houses the parched yellow of a van Gogh painting. It looked like the fields all over East Anglia, like the fields around this house. Harvest has begun on the farms, but the combines now start up late in the evening to avoid the fiery heat of the day.

I first saw England in the summer of 1976. 'Where is the "green and pleasant land"?' I asked. Everywhere I went – St James's Park, Hyde Park, Hidcote and Kiftsgate – the land was as parched as the Mississippi Delta at high noon. The English were apologetic, but they, too, were mystified. 'Climate change' wasn't in their literature. 'Drought' was blamed, and, perilous as it was, a few years later it was only a memory. We now know better. For years we have been warned – by Sir David Attenborough, Greta Thunberg, Prince Philip, James Lovelock, Al Gore – prophets who have been treated like cranks as the real cranks have denied which way the wind is blowing.

Since I've been sitting at my desk, two news flashes have appeared on my screen. A 'baling' fire in Burgate on the Suffolk/Norfolk border, 15 minutes from our farm, 18 fire engines on the scene. And a more encouraging report: the smaller fire three miles away in Honington is 'now contained'. I can hear Kerry saying 'no place on earth is exempt' as I turn again to Berry: 'The Earth is what we all have in common.'

August 3, 2022

REASONS TO BE CHEERFUL

I'M settling down to gather my thoughts when my husband sticks his head around the door. 'Try and write something cheerful. Nobody needs reminding of all that is wrong with the world.' He may as well ask me to have a go at glossolalia. I know he's right. Times are hard, and it's unnecessary to spread the gloom, but I'm unlikely to speak in tongues. I'm an Episcopalian from a slender sliver of the Bible Belt whose communicants are incapable of undulation however profound our religious fervour.

All the same, as soon as I wrote 'Reasons to be Cheerful' I hit a lull. I was still waiting for a reason when an email appeared with one word in the subject line: SAD. I scrolled down and read that my favourite theologian and minister (ordained Presbyterian) had died. I've been a member of Frederick Buechner's flock for longer than I can remember, a flock that consists mostly of the readers of his books. My collection of 'Buechners' (pronounced BEEK-ner) is nestled between Berry (Wendell) and Blythe (Ronald). The other Bs occupy more shelf space because I tend to loan my Buechner (Fred) books. I think they must find good homes because they never come back.

My 'starter Beuchner' was a small memoir of his early days called *The Sacred Journey*. Deeply personal, intimate and wryly humorous, he uncovers how, against all odds, he became a writer. It began with a tragedy that was never expressed. On a Saturday morning in late fall, he and his brother woke up around sunrise. He was 10, his brother not quite eight. Too early to get up, they play with a toy roulette wheel they've been given, staying put until they hear the rest of the house moving. They are aware that their father opens the door and looks in on them, but he says nothing. Neither do they. The next memory is the sound of shouting, 'a crazy parody of excitement'. After checking on his sons, their father had gone down to the family garage, turned on the engine of the car, and waited for the exhaust fumes to end his life.

Several days passed before a note was found. Written in pencil on the last page of *Gone with the Wind*, which was published that year (1936), it was addressed to his wife. 'I adore and love you and am no good… Give Freddy my watch. Give Jamie my pearl pen. I give you all my love.'

The note was placed where only his wife was likely to find it. In the last weeks of his life, he kept saying that something was wrong with the Chevy's exhaust system, in hopes that his life insurance would be validated. In the middle of the perilous uncertainty of the Depression, that may have been his last hope. It wasn't paid. Suicide was considered shabby and shameful – and illegal. There was no funeral, and their mother took the boys off to pre-war Bermuda, an escape where they lived an ecstatic few years before the start of the Second World War. It was also a time when the rules of 'Don't talk, don't trust, don't feel' were planted. For years afterwards, when asked how his father died, he would say heart trouble. 'A child takes life as it comes because he has no other way of taking it.'

If you've made it this far, you may be wondering when I am getting to the cheerful bit. It may not be the 'laugh-out-loud' feeling my husband was asking for. When I can't figure out how the world got into the mess it's in – or how we get out of it – I remember Beuchner. An evening spent reading him – often, his book *Whistling in the Dark: a Doubter's Dictionary* – removes me from the speed and fury of the news, the carnage of war, the devastation of fire and flood, the escalating costs of everything, the fields too hard to sow seed. Reading feels less evasive than Netflix and Riesling as a way of dealing with feeling the world is doomed.

Not that I always go to the bookshelf for rescue. In one of those late-night rambles on my laptop, I once came across an interview with Buechner on YouTube. He was asked his thoughts on the all-pervasive catch-all 'I'm spiritual, but not religious'. He didn't grimace at that tired old cliché. 'Faith is homesickness. Faith is a lump in the throat. It is sensing a presence. It isn't buying an argument.'

He admitted that 'to be religious is hard. I try to give Doubt and Darkness an equal role'. He then confessed he rarely goes to church. 'When I do I'm often bored and appalled, and then appalled that I'm appalled.'

A theologian who is not embarrassed about not having the answers cheers me up. In the same interview, he said that he often thought that 'getting ordained was a bad career move. Eyes glaze over when people hear that'. They might feel differently if they read his books. Writing the day after he died, the *New York Times* columnist David Brooks described Buechner as a 'borderstalker: too literary for Christians and too Christian for the literary set'.

Brooks echoes Reynolds Price, the writer who introduced me to Beuchner with his review in 1982 praising *The Sacred Journey*. Price wrote that 'spiritual autobiography suffered from too much spirituality and too little biography', citing that 'Augustine's "confessions" confess far too little and sermonise too much'.

I apologise for not doing better on the 'cheerful' front. In my defence, I'd say that when a man as generous, profound, inspiring and truthful as Buechner gives the world a literary ministry of nearly 40 books that show the way to 'talk, trust and feel', it's something to cheer. And when that man lives to the age of 96, how can we be sad?

Naturally, he put it rather better. 'What's lost is nothing to what's found,' he wrote, 'and all the death that ever was, set next to life, would scarcely fill a cup.'

September 7, 2022

TRADING PLACES

MY ancestral home – white columns, a veranda that stretched the width of the front, a row of rocking chairs – was knocked down. The new owners built a bigger and better house. They didn't put the new house in the exact same spot, but 'sited' it in the middle of the pecan orchard. By taking out four rows of pecan trees, they created an instant mature avenue that led right up to their new and grand veranda.

My sister and our cousin never got over it. When I said I thought the new house looked wonderful, they howled like wolverines. They would have stopped talking to me, but Southerners can never stop talking and that includes me. I reminded them that the house they loved was not like Tara in *Gone with the Wind*, that the veranda was so decrepit that you could only sit in the rocking chairs if you were blood kin and knew how to navigate safely the mosaic of rotten boards. I hinted that the columns weren't Doric; no laurel leaves were carved in the pediments.

One symptom of the Homesick Blues is memory

loss. I reckon they have forgotten that the house shook during tornados, was only heated downstairs and was cooled in sick-hot summers with an attic fan that was made for a cotton gin and sounded like a freight train rumbling through the night. After Uncle Ham built chicken houses on the back 40, we could never fill a bathtub deeper than 2in. Even when that entrepreneurial endeavour failed to prosper, and the chickens departed, the water pressure never recovered.

Although Americans claim to be appalled by the English religion of primogeniture, my grandmother left the house and farm to her son. When his sister – my Mama – found out, she went wild. She, too, suffered from homesick memory lapse: her favourite line was Thomas Wolfe's title *You Can't Go Home Again*, which she turned into her theme song, belting it out in her bourbon-rich Ella Fitzgerald voice. 'It's not a case of attachment,' she claimed when the will was revealed. 'It's just common decency.'

Long before the will surfaced, the family had metastasised from 'the home place'. Her son and heir – my Uncle Sidney – was a publisher living in Massachusetts, her daughter was living in Washington DC, and her grand-daughters were spread out in California, Maryland and England. The last member of the family to live in the house was my Uncle Jimmy. When he died, Aunt Ruby moved across the road, sold my Great-Aunt Edna's house (it was carried off on a flat-bed truck to a town 10 miles away) and built her own brand-new house. 'Everything works,' she says. 'It doesn't even shake when there's a tornado, but I sleep in the bathtub to be safe.'

If you wonder why I'm telling you all this, it's because we have a little 'home drama' going on in this family. It's not the Carlisle ancestral home, but Vineyard Cottage, two ancient farmworkers' cottages that were knocked into one 50 years ago. The cottage began life on the edge of a south-facing slope that burned every crop in a hot summer. Now, it looks out over nine acres of grapevines that thrive in the heat. For the past six years, it has been home to our son and daughter-in-law. It's now time to trade places.

In *Downton Abbey*, the Queen Anne dower house looks pretty swell, but in real life the largish houses created for the widows of the landowners have long since been sold off to pay Lloyd's, been converted into vital rental properties or now house the estate manager. Anything suitable for dowering at Wyken was sold in lean times, and during the 100 years of Carlisle occupation there's been no need for one. Two widows (1944, 1966) stayed put in the hall, and the third – my mother-in-law – much preferred her flat in Kensington.

More to the point, there's been a sea change. We are all living longer. The husband and wife now go together, allowing the young to move into the Big House when they have the energy, imagination – and jobs – needed to take it on.

I know lots of good 'trading places'. Friends in the next village knocked down a bungalow and built a dreamy house we call Le Temple de la Gloire. In Scotland, friends are moving into newly converted stables. A reimagined farmhouse in Cumbria distils a lifetime of taste and creativity and gives our friends the privacy their great house denied them.

Meanwhile, we are having a little tug-of-war over Vineyard Cottage. It's charming. It also has no foundation, no insulation, cracked chimneys and ceilings that were suitable for under-nourished farm workers. Admittedly, it has benefited from some excellent tenants in the past. The renowned and *mouvementé* American chef Robert Carrier made it a late-in-life posting, put in a beautiful kitchen, including a handsome Lacanche stove, and filmed 20 cooking episodes here. Then, aged 75, he returned to his first love: France. Another tenant put down stone floors and installed a claw-foot bath.

The poetic cottage is a stage set. Everything needs replacing: wiring, plumbing, roof. I study *Homebuilding & Renovating* magazine, and say things like 'consider the structural integrity of the building', 'rebuilding from scratch usually costs less' and 'no VAT on labour and building materials'.

I have the zeal of the pioneer, but I live in a world of *nostalgie de la boue*. My husband lived in the cottage for five years when he came back to run the farm. My son and daughter-in-law love its history – perhaps not the diminutive rooms, low ceilings and windows that whistle in the wind. I dream of my twilight years where 'everything works', is environmentally moral, warm in winter, cool in summer. As for my plans for a veranda as wide as six rows of cotton, and the avenue of pecan trees that will lead the way to the new house among the vines, I'm not saying a word.

October 5, 2022

ANTHEM OF OUR CRAZY AGE

MY old friend Ena planned every detail of her funeral. When she told me that she had written the eulogy to be delivered by her daughter, I said: 'Don't you think that's cheating?' 'No!' she snapped. 'I want to set the record straight. I was a very good mother!'

When the day arrived, the dutiful daughter read her mother's script. Word for word. I don't remember Katie looking up once. What I've never forgotten was the exit music: Edith Piaf's *Non, je ne regrette rien*.

I could see the humour in her choice. Luckily, I prefer Piaf to Sinatra, and I think we've all had enough of *I did it my way*. It required rather more effort for me to see the funny side at the wake back at the house, when we were served Prosecco. After she was diagnosed with her fast-moving cancer, Ena asked me to get four cases of Champagne from the Wine Society for her 'Kingdom Here I Come' party. 'Your Champagne!' Katie said. 'Mother called it her Twilight Wine. She claimed it was the only thing that agreed with her. She ordered the Prosecco from Tesco last month, insisting the "hangers on" wouldn't know the difference.'

Ena's exit plan included her property and chattels. When her son and daughter met with her solicitor, they learned that the family home was a sliver of its former self, as Ena had gone the full hog of equity release. 'We weren't banking on a grand inheritance,' admitted Katie, a primary-school teacher who, like her brother, an expert on lemurs, radiates pure goodness. It's one of those miracles that defies science: they are self-made people who show no trace of their gene pool.

I don't always think of Ena when Prosecco is served, but I do when I hear *Je ne regrette rien*. It's no longer a song that reminds me of rainy nights in Paris and black-and-white movies with Jean Gabin smoking Gauloises. Now, it makes me want to howl, because it has become the anthem of our crazy age. I don't blame the world of 'social media', where you can be an anonymous rat, spread suicidal despair and feel no remorse. This Age of No Remorse pre-dates Snapchat. I reckon it has litigious origins. Remorse triggers guilt triggers litigation. If you open your car door without looking and knock someone off their bike, you're advised not to apologise. Pity about the unlucky cyclist's bloody mouth, but keep quiet. You'll be paying with your back teeth if you admit carelessness.

You probably see where this is going. Straight to the politicians we elect to lead our country. No matter what trembling uncertainty they create in people's lives, no matter how many trees they uproot, how much hope and faith they crush, how many dreams they deny – they simply can't say 'I'm sorry'. Even the apologies wrung from them are minimalist mutterings, formulaic passwords carefully constructed to give them a free pass. Big crimes and small crimes, the mantra is 'He/she apologised' – an abbreviated use of language that is a 'get-out-of-hell-free' card and enables the confessor to continue roaming through the corridors of their crimes.

I admit I cried when Ali MacGraw died at the end of *Love Story*, but I knew the film's famous line – 'Love means never having to say you're sorry' – was ridiculous. I couldn't believe the Yale classicist who wrote it kept it in his second draft. In my experience, love means it's a good idea to say you're sorry with some frequency and look your chosen one in the eye as you say it.

Once she took to drink, Ena of No Regrets had the maternal skills of a sniper. Luckily, her children – and most of her friends – were old enough to get out of the way. The damage done by elected leaders who cock up and let down their country is another story. Regular folk can't get out of the way so easily. Leaders owe it to those who chose them – and those who did not choose them – to say they are sorry when they have made choices that turned out to be wrong.

I've often wondered if the light and sound of history would have been different if, instead of announcing he would not seek re-election, Lyndon Johnson had told the American people that the Vietnam War could not be won. That the deceptions, fabrications, deliberate distortions were made by decision-makers who didn't know what they were talking about.

The same confession could be made by the youthful prime minister who led his country into a war in Iraq. And, what if the disenchanting prime minister who 'gave' us a referendum had said 'I've got to make this work' instead of walking away with a cheery whistle?

As for the stream of prime ministers standing around in Downing Street lately, did the Latin scholar say 'Mea culpa, mea culpa, I got this wrong'? Did anyone say 'I said it was a piece of cake, but it turned out to be a quagmire'? Or 'I said it would be £10 billion and it is going to be £400 billion'? Did you hear 'I betrayed your faith in me and I am sorry'?

Regret seems to be about the loss of face, loss of privileges, loss of salary, car and driver. Remorse is something altogether different. It may not patch up the damage, the mess, the pain, the disappointment, but it is a form of solace. It doesn't end our primal rage and cynical despair, but it helps to humanise the powerful and comfort the powerless.

A new prime minister has moved into Downing Street. Is it really the fourth in three years? It feels like the eloquent Mr Johnson (Samuel) describing second marriages: 'The triumph of hope over experience.'

Trepidation nibbles at my heart, but I live in hope. We know there are hard times ahead – as Tennyson said of Camelot, 'The realm has gone to wrack' – and I'm keeping my hopes modest. I hope never again to hear *'Hasta la vista*, baby', but *Je regrette beaucoup* works for me.

November 2, 2022

A DAY OF PEACE IN THE MIDST OF WAR

THANKSGIVING has come and gone. I love this quieter, familial prelude to Christmas, a minimalist gathering based on family, friends and food, with emphasis on cornbread stuffing, not on stuff.

I say 'quieter', but, until her dying day, my grandmother believed that the fourth Thursday in November was a 'Yankee holiday' because it was Abraham Lincoln who, in 1863, proclaimed it an official holiday. She inherited her father's belief that the President's call for a 'day of peace in the midst of war' celebrated the Union victory at Gettysburg.

Papa (pronounced Pawpaw), my agnostic grandfather, born the year that Lincoln was shot, would remind her that George Washington created the 'day of prayer and Thanksgiving' back in 1789, but Papa had his own objections. A Jeffersonian, he believed that calls for prayer to a higher power didn't sit well in a nation based on the separation of church and state. Even his brothers, four Baptist preachers who joined us for dinner, had to keep quiet, and the blessing was relegated to the youngest grandchild.

The all-time winner in the Grace Stakes was our cousin Jamie's prayer, aged four: 'God is great, God is good. God, I hope this food is good.'

That prayer was always answered. I feel reverential about the menu: New England chowder, followed by the Norfolk Black turkey pan-smoked over grape vines, sweet-potato casserole, cornbread dressing and giblet gravy. My gospel is 'Save Room For Pie', and I like a slice each of pumpkin and pecan, with a little ice cream to cut the sweetness.

My memories of Thanksgivings Past aren't all seen through a soft lens. For years, I ranted about 'cock-eyed patriotism' that ignored the Wampanoag Indians whose humane goodness kept the Pilgrims from starving. A whole decade was spent in battles over civil rights and the war in Vietnam. When bourbon is added to a family gathering of Southerners, you have to question Faulkner's belief that 'Civilisation began with fermentation'. Civility melts faster than butter when you mix politics with Jack Daniel's.

And yet, such is our human need to be together, the ritual of our annual gathering wins out. I don't envy families who have strict Rules – 'No Trump', 'No Hillary', 'No fracking', 'No swearing' and 'No whining' at the dinner table – but it must work, because they get together every Thanksgiving.

Still, it's a hard year not to brood. The war in Ukraine has turned an old dove like me into a crazy hawk. The thought of autocracies outnumbering liberal democracies keeps me awake at night. A rich country where families rely on food banks, teenagers are stabbed in the streets, and the oldest and most noble democracy on earth turns into the Theatre of the Absurd: who can ignore this? It goes on: China. Afghanistan. Nuclear weapons. Floods and fires. Despite all resolve for optimism, I worry we're doomed when I think of Elon Musk/Kanye West/ *The Crown*/cryptocurrency. How does this end?

One year, a great-aunt suggested everyone at the table tell one thing that had happened over the year that they were grateful for. It felt straight out of *Reader's Digest*, but bad manners to refuse. After an awkward silence, my grandmother announced – in front of my new English husband – 'I'm just so glad Carla finally got married.' A cousin quickly belted out her gratitude: 'My DIVORCE was final in June!' The best was Aunt Sissy's daughter, who whispered: 'I was saved by AA and HRT.'

This morning I was still wading in the muddy waters of memory when I heard a vaguely familiar voice on the radio. It was a clip from Franklin Roosevelt's famous *Four Freedoms* speech in 1941. The BBC is celebrating its centenary year with Radio 4's Reith Lectures featuring four thinkers exploring the four themes: freedom of speech; freedom of worship; freedom from want; freedom from fear.

I grew up with that speech. Not listening to the President on the radio, but in classrooms where the posters of Norman Rockwell's paintings inspired by the four freedoms reminded children born after the war how lucky we were to be American. Half a century after they were painted, I saw the originals in the Dulwich Picture Gallery in London.

Rockwell was America's best-known artist when he painted the 'Four Freedoms' to raise money for the war effort. The Office of War Information turned them down as 'not suitable for government use'. When *The Saturday Evening Post* launched a publicity campaign with them in 1943 as the Second World War raged, the government changed its mind and printed millions of posters of the paintings. In one, a family is gathered around the table as the turkey arrives. It represents 'Freedom from Want'. It's called *Thanksgiving*. Sentimental they may be, but the paintings were meant to show Americans what they were fighting for. What would a Rockwell paint today? Six workers at Walmart, shot in cold blood in Thanksgiving week? The homeless living in tents on the streets of San Francisco, lining up for turkey dinners in a supermarket car park?

I'm writing this before the lectures are broadcast, but I suspect the 'thinkers' will tell us eloquently what we already know: that the precious four freedoms are in reverse.

Meanwhile, this year, my Thanksgiving 'gratitude' list wasn't a nervous silence. My sister, brother-in-law and our cousin Jamie came here the week before. We haven't been together since pre-lockdown days. My sister has stage-four lung cancer, but is in remission, thanks to a medical miracle called Keytruda. She's slower, but she's still bossy and courageous, and she managed to fit in *Hamilton*, Evensong at St Paul's and a lot of eating, drinking and talking. She was determined to meet the newest member of the family: her grandniece, my first grandchild, born October 1. We defied Pawpaw's non-sectarian wishes, and our first Thanksgiving together in 20 years was blessed by cousin Jamie.

Yep, the same one whose blessing, aged four, still makes us laugh. We reckon it was prophetic: she's now an ordained Episcopal priest. You could call it 'amazing grace'.

December 7, 2022

VII
Way Over Yonder

LOVE IN THE RUINS

ALTHOUGH I am a member of the New Year: Stay Home tribe, I enter a new year with respect. I choose a rare and irreplaceable bottle of wine, I prepare a perfect fillet of venison and celeriac gratin, and lay a table for two in front of the fire. This year – no trains, no nurses, no post, no ambulances and a bad war – I think, but don't say, that a general anaesthetic might have been a better choice than Pauillac.

And so the year begins. The sheep welcome me as their Angel of the Bales (hay) and Buckets (ewe nuts). The chickens and turkeys no longer try to escape their wired world when I arrive with their oats and corn. Once a Palais des Poulets, their prison is now called 'Love in the Ruins'. In Walker Percy's book of that title, a doctor creates a miraculous instrument, an 'ontological lapsometer', a kind of stethoscope of the human spirit. The doctor plans to use it to cure mankind's spiritual flu, and save the world from destruction. A cure for bird flu, a cure for spiritual flu – how do we get there?

Accepting the uncontrollable vagaries of time and change enabled me to stop making New Year resolutions a few decades ago. Instead, I undertake what I call 'The Clearances'. Some years, it's simply taking the bottles to the glass recycling next to the grain store. I stack newspapers filled with articles on how to achieve balance, strength and weight loss in the paper skip. I don't believe these little acts will save the planet, but they treat the symptoms of spiritual flu when no cure is in sight.

This year, the New-Year mission began back in August, when we read Giles Coren's column 'Bin those books, your children will thank you'. It was like an O. Henry short story: I read it online and printed it out for my husband. He read the print edition and tore it out for his wife (me). Although the books on our shelves have never intermarried ('That's mine!'), we share nuggets of truth. Mr Coren's bibliocide message inspired rare complicity. We agreed to bin our books, which really means: 'Edit your one and precious life. Prepare for Judgement Day. Do it *Now*.' And, five months later, as 2023 crept in, we began.

In fact, we aren't motivated by the afterlife gratitude of our son and daughter-in-law. We are more troubled by the idea that they will simply load the thousands of books into the John Deere tractor and trailer and dump the load at an Oxfam warehouse. Or, if there is a red-diesel shortage, dump the books into the pit on a field, together with rotten bales and centuries of agricultural debris.

Our fears have roots. We inherited an ancestral library of hefty volumes on field sports, cricket, farming in Argentina, flower arranging, lives of Field Marshal Haig. With no tender regret, we sold the lot to a specialist bookseller from Aldeburgh (they still existed back then). We cleared the attic, but, alas, we did not clear the shelves in the rooms where our own books live.

Now, almost all the second-hand bookshops have closed (except for Oxfam). There is still a wonderful book stall in the market square in Cambridge, but they don't want paperbacks, modern fiction, crime or Habitat coffee-table books. They prefer cookbooks published in 1895 to ones published in 1995, and encyclopaedias, textbooks and Bibles have no commercial future at all.

The 'P' word is often heard. One of the large second-hand booksellers in America, Wonder Books, pulps 'damaged' books, producing 100,000lb a month of recycled paper. I don't dare ask what Oxfam does with its unsellable books. Are the unwanted tomes sent to Rwanda? Are volumes of *The Da Vinci Code* sent to countries ravaged by climate change? Do the starving and homeless read old Lonely Planet guides by candlelight, using *Gone with the Wind* for firewood? And here's a spoiler alert: hardback books can't be recycled – glued bindings contaminate rivers. It seems that books aren't good for the earth.

Do we blame Amazon, which made it easier to acquire books than to go to the local library? Or (*mea culpa*), blame IKEA and the Billy bookshelves? Or do we just accept the security and comfort in the volumes, read and unread, that furnish our lives?

So it was that Epiphany began at Wyken Hall with a stack of black boxes from Anglia Produce. Strong enough to transport swedes, turnips and beetroots, they are now filled with His and Her books. Despite a long and happy marriage, our library is 'Separate but Equal' and we conduct our bound farewells accordingly. We plan for the boxes to reside in the old farm workshop and to emerge on sunny days at the farmers' market to be sold. Proceeds may be meagre, but they will go to the Ixworth Library in the neighbouring village.

When I had filled five boxes (goodbye John Updike, Margaret Drabble, Iris Murdoch, Robert Lowell), I made myself a mug of coffee and retrieved the *FT Weekend* from the recycling pile. I began to read an interview with Annie Proulx (rhymes with 'new'). She described her recent move from the Pacific Northwest, where she'd developed an allergy to western red cedar, to New Hampshire in New England. She says that the hardest part of her move was 'winnowing down' her beloved library because she could not afford the third moving truck taking the books would have required. 'I thought I could do without them', but, when she got to her new home and unpacked, she realised 'the enormity of what I had done. I was filled with book grief'.

The words 'book grief' struck at my heart. Without a lapsometer to cure my 'spiritual flu', the thought of adding 'book grief' to my list of sorrows makes me feel crazy. I've just spent a desolate hour looking for my old copy of *Love in the Ruins*. I fear the new year is passing me by.

January 4, 2023

THE COURAGE TO BE HAPPY

MARRIAGE and columns have this in common: you tend to repeat yourself. More than once in these pages I have quoted *The New Yorker*'s legendary film critic Pauline Kael, but here I go again. After President Nixon's landslide victory in 1972, she wrote: 'I live in a rather special world. I don't personally know anyone who voted for Nixon.'

I also live in a rather special world. I don't personally know anyone who has bought a book called *Spare*. I can go further. I have a small bookshop. Located in the old milking parlour, it is literary, personally curated and financially the most viable of our various farm diversifications. Readers will not find copies of *Spare* in my bookshop. Charlotte – who does the ordering – and I never even discussed it. Instead, we ordered 10 copies of *Orwell on Truth*, and declined the opportunity to stock the 'bestseller of all time'.

Which doesn't mean that this farm – with its fields of wheat and barley, vineyard, restaurant, Shetland sheep, weekly farmers' market and miles of beetle banks – is a veritable hamlet of censorship and sensibility. I ceaselessly plough the black-and-white world of print. I confess that I have now read thousands of inches of reviews of the Prince's – and his creative ghostwriter J. R. Moehringer's – memoir with a compulsion that embarrasses me to admit. I have been gripped by the sheer brilliance of some of the reviews (my list of the best includes Philip Hensher in *The Spectator*, Tina Brown (naturally) in *The Sunday Times*, Sarah Sands in the *FT*). I read with the gnawing guilt of a fugitive.

Any moral high ground I occupied for not watching the Netflix programmes was diminished when I succumbed to the ITV interview with Tom Bradby. It was exhausting, although I found Mr Bradby even-handed. I also thought Harry had been coached by a pro. He had his lines down pat.

As I trawled through the reviews, I could hear my grandmother's voice. If she saw me reading *Seventeen/Glamour* or, worse still, *Cosmopolitan*, she accused me of 'going slumming'. She regularly snapped 'You aren't obliged to read trash!' and handed me Jane Austen or Willa Cather. Her reproofs have been long lasting. I never read or watch 'trash' without the itch of guilt. I also suspect that *Pride and Prejudice* led me to England. It may even have paved the path to my lucky tenancy at *Country Life*, where, back on May 2, 2018, I welcomed Meghan Markle into the sisterhood of American women married to Englishmen. It was a hopeful and happy time. The heart of the country was full.

Those days now feel like Once Upon a Time. I'm worn out from buckin' and snortin' with my fellow Americans who have watched *The Crown* (I didn't) and Oprah and bought into the story that the English – and the Royal Family – were eaten up by their prejudice against the new royal bride. I'll say it again: I may live in a rather special world, but I don't personally know anyone who didn't welcome the exciting new era of Harry and Meghan. And if one image of that wedding stands out above all others, it will forever be the heart-wrenching moment of Prince Charles walking his son's bride down the aisle.

We are now left with questions that feel like sifting sand: what do the Sussexes want? How does this painful saga end? I have no idea what the Sussexes want, of course. Nobody does. My more cynical friends (English) believe the Duchess wants to be Michelle Obama and the Duke wants to be the brave Zelensky and bring about world peace by destroying his personal Putin: the UK tabloid press. Good luck with that. My sweet cousin (American) has a gentler take: 'Now that they have spurted out all their unhappiness, I hope they will have the courage to be happy.'

It's quite a thought: the courage to be happy. To the modern ear it sounds a little too self-helpy, but

I wish that there was someone to advise the Duke and Duchess that there is no future in a career of chewing over the bitterness of things. Bitterness – and its twin, Hate – leads to a kind of madness. It corrodes reconciliation.

If I could give advice, would I try the modern mantra of 'lighten up'? Unlikely. I hate to be told to lighten up. Would I tell them that happiness depends on the courage to forget, the courage to forgive? I don't know. Although Oprah and I were born 50 miles apart and we both grew up in a world where inspirational verses were posted on church billboards, I emerged with a lifelong allergy to platitudes.

The best I could come up with are a few dos and don'ts. Don't read the tabloids and stuff online because nobody in your rather special world does – at least, no one you know personally and care about. Do look at what is going on in the world around you. It's a cruel world, and you have a reprieve, one that only money can buy. Do consider what Elizabeth II understood in her bones: that the greatest courage is to be silent. And rewind the film of your wedding day. Understand that outpouring of gaiety and love and hope. Remember.

Meanwhile, in honour of the grandmother who did her utmost to steer me away from trashy reading, I'm taking a break from writers writing on *Spare*, even the ones that begin 'Spare me'. I'm reading another book she put in my hands, Edith Wharton's novella *The Last Asset*. It has words of advice that have served me well:

'There are lots of ways of being miserable, but there's only one way of being comfortable, and that is to stop running round after happiness. If you make up your mind not to be happy there's no reason why you shouldn't have a fairly good time.'

February 1, 2023

HOME ON THE RANGE

WE were halfway into series two before it dawned on us. Except for the Lamborghini tractor and the magical bank balance, Diddly Squat – Clarkson's Farm – and Wyken Farm (rhymes with 'lickin') are two versions of the same story, with one big difference: West Suffolk's council was pro-farmers, in favour of jobs for local folks, and had common sense.

If you aren't watching *Clarkson's Farm*, the television series that folks in these parts find more compulsive than *Happy Valley*, you may wonder what I'm talking about. My subject is farming, something that resembles country life and provides ambience for *Country Life*, but is now in bad trouble. That's the message Jeremy Clarkson, my contender for 'Britain's most cherished farmer', has set out to show people in this country. A late-in-life farmer, he wants to save farms, starting with his own 1,000 acres in the Cotswolds.

When I married a Suffolk farmer in the 1980s, my dowry comprised a middle-aged labrador and an apocalyptic vision of farming. 'Diversification is

Salvation!' I whispered on our honeymoon. *And in those heady early days of married love, the farmer believed his wife and they went forth.* In common with Mr Clarkson and his fearless Irish Lisa, neither of us could reverse a tractor out of the farmyard, but we were blessed with benign optimism and dreamy ignorance.

My Suffolk farmer also had 1,000 acres, with one south-facing slope: sandy loam over chalk, this slope burned up every crop in a hot summer. The bride had a hankering for viticulture, although my knowledge chiefly consisted of having lived in France and reading Hugh Johnson's *World Atlas of Wine*. Knowing what's in your glass is not the same as recognising the difference between a grapevine and a honeysuckle, but I was determined to make French-style wines and save the farm. I planted Chardonnay and Pinot Noir *pour ajouter un peu de noblesse* to the vineyard, and, at the urging of Paris vigneron Lucien Legrand, planted a few early-ripening varieties.

Like Mr Clarkson, I was on fire with commercial verve. My mantra was 'to make wine you have to sell wine'. Visitors gazed in awe at our 400-year-old tithe barn. Farmers saw a barn too small for modern machinery, but a useful dumping ground for potato boxes and old feed bags. I saw a vineyard restaurant, winery and shop.

'You'll never get planning permission' said the first architect before he disappeared. Our local builder said what we needed was an architectural engineer, and, together, we came up with a proposal. Planning was granted first time around.

Another bit of luck. Although over-educated, I had only one tangible skill: I'd worked in restaurants during and after university. One of those stints was at Chez Panisse, in Berkeley, California. Now famous as the first 'farm-to-table' restaurant, in my day it was very French, with the emphasis on seasonal ingredients from local farms. I wanted to bring that 'seasonal and local' ethos to Wyken.

It's hard to believe now that this was considered revolutionary. However, my plan for the kitchen garden to produce the vegetables for the restaurant wasn't feasible. We'd have had to triple its size. We now grow herbs, salads, sorrel and flowers and buy in the rest from local growers. Always on the menu is our own wild venison, asparagus in spring and, of course, our own wine.

And, sometimes, our small, companionable and hardy Shetland sheep. We breed the ewes, and the ram lambs are eaten as hoggets at 18 months old. It's a good story. It's not the true story. With a part-time shepherd and ewe nuts and hay provided in winter, the sheep lose £10,000 a year, a figure that is the source of some marital discord.

Not quite up there are the Red Polls, a more serious disruption to familial harmony. The dairy herd at Wyken was sold in the 1960s, but, like Mr Clarkson,

I thought Suffolk Red Polls would yield steaks and authenticity for the restaurant. I considered the cows 'my' herd. I didn't know they would escape, poach the lawns and rack up stupendous vet bills. When we came to eat Rufus, our first calf, my farm-to-table commitment began to wane. My cows went to a farm in Essex.

Of course, I have 'my' chickens. They are layers, and only required to provide eggs, so *coq au vin* is not an issue. A domestic flock, the eggs can't be sold. Oak Farm nearby supplies the restaurant and the egg stall on our farm drive.

Got that? *Egg stall*. Not 'farm shop'. Farm shops are as tempting to farmers as mud is to pigs, but they're a hard row to hoe. Think shelf life, minimal mark-up, wastage, supermarket competition. Instead, we started a weekly farmers' market on the farm. Now 20 years old, it provides all the fun of a farm shop without the headache. And we have a 'country store', where we sell our wines, including our sparkling wine, Wyken Moonshine, and our Good Dog Ale made with our own barley. We also sell Irish and Scottish woollens, watering cans, shovels, dog beds, jackets like Monty Don wears, Suffolk pottery and, in the old dairy, books. The most absurd of the official dictates to Mr Clarkson: he isn't allowed to sell his *own* books at Diddly Squat because they weren't produced within a 16-mile radius. Good lord.

This year, we celebrated the 30th anniversary of our farm restaurant, 25 years in *The Good Food Guide*, and 24 years as a Michelin Bib Gourmand. This farm has survived Lloyd's, foot-and-mouth, floods, droughts and the pandemic. The jury is still out on farming post-Brexit, and who knows what Defra's 'public good' means – kill cows, but protect badgers? However, we have 45 people on our payroll: chefs, waiters, gardeners, shop staff, cleaners, carpenter – and one genuine farmer. Thirty years ago, this farm was on life support. It now thrives, mostly. I hope it gives the West Oxfordshire District Council food for thought. Meanwhile, *Bon courage*, Diddly Squat. Fight on!

March 1, 2023

SLOUCHING TOWARDS BETHLEHEM

MILESTONES are like hailstones: their arrival comes as a surprise, but they melt away quickly. I've now lived in England twice as long as I lived in the land of my birth. I'm the wife of a man born in Wales, the mother of a son born in the Hammersmith Hospital, and a British passport is nestled in my sock drawer. I think I sound as English as Dame Judi Dench, but I rarely meet a stranger who doesn't ask 'Where are you from?'

First-time visitors to the garden look surprised when they see a row of wooden rocking chairs spread across the fictional veranda. They think it's exotic to sit and rock and gaze at the sheep in the meadow. What's missing from this Southern tableau is the percussion of screen doors slamming. I'd bet my last nickel that climate change will convert the English to the miracle that lets in the air and keeps out the flies. And another Southern essential: fans. Towards the end of his life, my father came to live with us. Almost his last words of wisdom were: 'I know the English don't believe in air conditioning, but this house needs some ceiling fans.' We now sit under the memorial fans. They stir the air and calm the spirit in this house that is older than America.

My father died expecting to wake up in the night and require a selection of reading matter. His deathbed companions were John Grisham, P. D. James and W. B. Yeats, citizens of three different countries bound by a common language. I spent that summer reading those three volumes with the crazy hope of a shipwrecked sailor looking for a message in a bottle. I no longer remember the Grisham or the James, but, last weekend, the Yeats poem came back to me.

As I watched in horror a small Mississippi Delta town called Rolling Fork being wiped off the face of the earth by a 200mph tornado, I could hear the voice of my father speaking the lines:

> Turning and turning in the widening gyre
> The falcon cannot hear the falconer...

How can we hear the falconer in an age when we are witnesses to daily horror shows of devastation? We've lived through two years of body counts from a pandemic, and a year-long tragedy of destruction wrought on Ukraine, the shock at that war interrupted by scenes of the earthquake in Turkey and Syria. If we're deaf to the falconer, it is our guilty instinct for survival.

The tornado feels personal. I was born 75 miles

from that small town, but this is not the Mississippi I left behind. For a start, the soft-spoken mayor of Rolling Fork is a black man called Eldridge Walker. Most of the citizens of these Delta towns, the poorest towns in the poorest state in America, are black, but in the South of my youth the notion of meaningful racial integration, beginning with the right to vote, was under attack. There were no black mayors because there were no black voters. Mr Walker is also the funeral director, a position in a Southern town that ranks in dignity and significance above mayor. It's progress, but not a miracle.

Even in this impoverished small town, there are two schools. In 1970, one year after the Supreme Court ordered the desegregation of schools, the Sharkey-Issaquena Academy was founded, a private, non-sectarian school. Almost every town, however small, however poor, has a private (white) academy. The racial impasse – what my father called 'the agony of the soul' – is not over.

I was still staring at scenes of the deadly tornado when another Southern scene pushed Rolling Fork into the background: a shooting in a primary school in Nashville, Tennessee, three nine year olds dead, three teachers dead. And this time, the shooter is dead. I hear myself say 'Thank god', but who is not relieved when the bad guy with a gun is shot by a good guy with a gun? Especially when we remember how many were killed in Uvalde, Texas, last May, when a man with the AR-15 semi-automatic rifle killed 19 students and two teachers as the police lingered outside the school.

> Things fall apart; the centre cannot hold;
> Mere anarchy is loosed upon the world.

I love Nashville. I have cousins there: one a doctor at Vanderbilt University Hospital, another a country-western singer with two little girls under nine. Nashville is home to three writers I love – Ann Patchett, Margaret Renkl and Jon Meacham – and home of the country music I listen to in my kitchen late at night.

The city is also the capital of the state with some of the most permissive gun laws in the country. You don't need a permit to buy a gun in Tennessee, or a licence to own one. If you buy your gun from a private seller you don't even need a background check. The 28-year-old assailant in the primary-school shooting legally bought seven firearms from five local gun shops in the months before her killing spree, including an AR-15 semi-automatic rifle. One in 20 Americans owns an AR-15, which can fire 60 rounds a minute. That's faster than the speed of sound.

> The blood-dimmed tide is loosed, and everywhere
> The ceremony of innocence is drowned;

The South is a land of readers and writers. I may be wrong, but I suspect the Southerners who read Yeats don't tend to own semi-automatic rifles, and they send their children to a small school like Covenant Primary in the belief it will protect them from the stench of violence. These days have not made me homesick, only home-sad.

Turning to poetry can feel like a retreat as the world gets hotter, the tornados become more violent and the guns more powerful and plentiful, so that more people are killed in the shortest time. But the question must be asked:

> And what rough beast, its hour come round at last,
> Slouches towards Bethlehem to be born?

April 5, 2023

THE ONCE AND FUTURIST KING

I NEVER danced with a man who danced with a woman who danced with The Prince of Wales, but I have defended him through the years with a stubborn loyalty that resides in the world of black and white. Or, more accurately, exists in the archives of *Country Life*.

For instance, on June 26, 1997, I took issue in these pages with the vicar of St Mary the Virgin in Tetbury, Gloucestershire, who complained that The Prince of Wales did not attend church regularly enough. He accused The Prince of 'not appearing at an act of worship since February'. I welcomed the column inches to express my belief that one's spiritual life cannot be measured by church attendance. My theme was simple: The Prince's spiritual life is a private matter. I then deviated to more secular matters: his sartorial life. I love his beautifully tailored dense tweeds, his natural ease in a kilt, the perfect blue of his pinstripe suits, the waterproof authenticity of his country wardrobe.

By the time the *Bristol Evening Post*'s headline announced 'Tetbury Man to Wed', the deep divisions in this farming community following the Dimbleby and *Panorama* dramas had mostly died down. On the eve of their wedding, I wrote in these pages that the older and wiser Charles marrying the older and wiser Camilla felt like a victory for the steadier qualities of warmth, humour and understanding.

I then wandered off on a viticultural tangent, and compared marriage to pruning my vines. Pruning is the foundation for all that a grape grower does for the rest of the year. Every act, every choice, builds on what is left on the mature vine. A blend of rote and concentration. You don't know if there will be enough water to create juice, or enough sun to create sweetness. It is an act of faith.

And so the years have passed. Now that the battle lines of opinion about the new King are mostly confined to the realms of Netflix, you might think the coronation is a time to keep silence. However, I have one more little bone to pick. I'm worried that the British don't realise how lucky they are to have Charles III as their King.

Sensitive, thoughtful and wise, when he was barely 21 years old Charles was exploring the future with the focused eye of an ancient mapmaker. Shortly after his investiture as Prince of Wales in 1969, he gave his first major public speech to the Countryside Steering Committee for Wales. It was about river pollution, single-use plastic, car emissions. His presence that day was permeated with the past, but the young Prince set out a different stall: to construct a survival manual for the future.

Farmers, even those who haven't converted their farms to the full organic of Highgrove, know that Charles III is a kindred spirit. Our acres of wildflower meadows, our Shetland sheep who only appear on the menu as 'hogget', our rows of beetle banks and various breeds of chickens, are all in harmony with this man whose unquenchable resolution has made us better stewards of this sacred land.

Not only do I fear that this country doesn't appreciate its good luck at having this King, I'm worried about the republican fervour that wants Charles III to wear the crown and shut up. No 'black spider memos' (note: they were mostly typed, no black ink, extremely polite, nothing nefarious or controversial, only encouragement of common sense).

Will silencing The King's voice be a loss? Google the 'carbuncle' designs for the National Gallery that he lamented, and look at what we have instead. Look at Poundbury, and then witness the acres of identikit houses now flooding the countryside. Look at The Royal Drawing School (originally The Prince of Wales Drawing School). And, perhaps most remarkable of all, think of the million lives transformed by The Prince's Trust.

Then reflect on the politicians who want to shut

him up. Think about the speech that Charles III, second only to Sir David Attenborough as the resolute Voice of the Planet in the UK, was due to deliver at COP27 in Egypt in November 2022. Remember that Prime Minister Liz Truss gave the order for The King to stay home, a command upheld by her successor. To silence The King, especially on a subject about which he has spoken with humanity and knowledge for four decades, makes the UK look ridiculous.

Kingship is a mystery. It is obscure, enigmatic and almost beyond comprehension. I know that not all kings are noble, but Charles III is a futurist, forged in wisdom, common sense, courage and faith. He has slimmed down the cast of performing royals, and revealed his innate pragmatism in reducing the royal property portfolio. His moving speech in Barbados suggests that he is ready to remove his face from the postage stamps and pocket change of the remaining 14 realms, including Australia, Canada and New Zealand. This is a King who wants to save the planet, beginning with transforming his realm.

Although I never danced with The King, I have one small thing in common. As a lifelong lover of music and a champion of the Arts, His Majesty has planned every detail of the music for the coronation, including commissioning world-class composers. One commission from a trio of composers is based on a favourite hymn of The King's, 'Be Thou my

Vision'. It's a 'triptych for orchestra', with the opening movement by Nigel Hess.

When this free-born American married her Englishman in the Crypt Chapel at Westminster a few yards from where the coronation will take place, we commissioned a young composer to write a piece of music for our wedding. His name? Nigel Hess. It feels almost like dancing with The Prince of Wales, and I smile and rejoice at the thought.

May 3, 2023

ACKNOWLEDGEMENTS

LATE in life, Chekhov said that everything he read seemed to him 'not short enough'. I know the feeling but I can't make this shorter.

ANOTHER COUNTRY would never have happened without Mark Hedges, *Country Life*'s editor. He believed that looking at the world through the lens of a farm in Suffolk had a place amid the clutter and chaos of one century closing and a new one beginning and wanted to give it the more enduring acreage of a monthly essay. Mark has always given me extraordinary liberty to speak my mind. He is the kind of editor who is the writer's truest friend.

Kate Green sits in the control tower of *Country Life* in her cottage in the heart of Somerset. Week after week, she 'makes it happen'.

Writing is a solitary business but editing a proof is a duet. Octavia Pollock is my sub-editor, and her saintly patience and good sense is a vital part of my peace of mind. She tolerates more 'let me re-phrase that' and 'just one more tweak' than I dare to admit. No one else could put up with me.

Once upon a time 40 men and their families lived on this farm. Now there is one genuine farmer. Without Will Reed the farm would not have a soul.

When we converted our 400-year-old barn into a vineyard restaurant and country store, the young builder who masterminded the transformation was Trevor Pollard. He is Wyken's Atlas, saving every structure on this farm from collapse and keeping us upright, as Atlas did the sky.

With 50 people on the payroll this sounds like a Prize Day roll call, but without Roger Ingleton, officially the Accounts Manager but the one person who knows how everything works (biomass/broadband/solar panels/drains, the money), we'd be stuck. Sarah Patterson runs the country store with style and grace, and heads a team that are like family.

Modern farming spelled the end of farm communities. The weekly farmers' market at Wyken, started during the Foot and Mouth epidemic, thrives thanks to the tireless efforts of Anne-Marie Hornsblow. Our vineyard restaurant creates another kind of community, thanks to the talents of our chefs and the kindness of the front-of-house staff who provide happiness to thousands of visitors each year.

Pip Green's arrival as head gardener eight years ago was a miracle. Born in this corner of Suffolk, she spent 25 years working in gardens on the West Coast of America before coming back home. She's like a long-lost sister, and an outstanding plantswoman. And Alex Fricker, assistant gardener, loves everything mechanical. A garden needs two to tango.

Carlos Ledesma is our Ecuadorean boatbuilder and handyman. Every department vies for his time and skill. Angie Burrows' patience, perseverance and good humour has kept our hearth and home from descending into irreversible chaos. Happiness depends on the skill and goodness of others.

I never see enough of my friends but without them life in the country would be a lonely place. Helen and Alan Ward are Suffolk neighbours whose friendship, wit and warmth have given the whole Carlisle family the utmost happiness.

Life is too short to make old friends and I treasure mine: Valerie Wade, Marie Brenner, Virginia Graham, Mac Gordon, Kerry Forbes, Susan Tureen, David Sheppard, Judith Harris, Christopher Jordan, Ruth Watson, Peter Dawson, Stanley Bates and Michael Elles, Paul Evans and Suzanne Ludlow, Helen and Gilbert McCabe, Nicholas and Emma Brooksbank, Raymond O'Rourke, Michael Harvey.

My sister Jan, the cousinage of Jamie and Marguerite and the sisters I acquired in marriage – Christabel, Katharine and Barbara – make up the lucky tapestry of family.

Two 'old friends' I think of with more gratitude than they can ever know: Patty Piper who gave me

France, and David Blow who gave me England. They shared their love of two countries with me and enriched and changed my life.

That these transient essays are having a second life is thanks to Marion and Alan Marshall of Mascot Media. Without these intrepid publishers all the words would have bit the dust or, more likely, languished in old OKA boxes. Their skill, thoughtful guidance and amazing trust made this book happen.

The husband who quietly pleaded for more laughter in these essays had every right to. He has brought love and fun to Wyken and given me the happiest years of my life. A big part of the fun has been our son Sam who now lives in the vineyard with his wife Georgia. We have passed the torch and they are now running what we created here. They have also brought a new kind of joy to our lives: a baby girl called Ida Paloma Rose. I call her my Moon Pie and I am her Meemaw. If anything guarantees laughter, fun and hope in this crazy world, it's a yellow-headed lap baby.